The Last 18

Travis Mewhirter

Saguaro Books, LLC
SB
Arizona

Saguaro Books, LLC
16201 E. Keymar Dr.
Fountain Hills, AZ 85268
www.saguarobooks.com

ISBN: 978-1512131161
Library of Congress Cataloging Number
LCCN: 2015941015
Printed in the United States of America
First Edition

For my mother, Jill, the greatest woman I've ever met and the best mama a boy could ask for.

PROLOGUE

The course was empty, naked almost. I'd never seen it like this—so calm, so quiet, so serene, free of the drunks, the cursers and the incessant hum of the golf carts.

The last time I had been here, at the world famous Olympiad Golf Club, there were towering grandstands behind the greens packed to capacity, throngs of people there to watch me play. The fairways had been lined with spectators, stretching and craning their necks, hoisting their children on their shoulders, to watch as I marched down the fairway with my younger brother, Brian.

But now, there wasn't a single soul. And, that was exactly how I wanted it.

A cool, San Diego breeze whispered through the palms as I strolled down the first fairway where I was once, just a couple shots off the lead with seventeen holes left to play.

I was just seventeen years old at the time, hadn't even had a taste of college and, yet, was fearless. My younger brother, who had never been nervous about a tournament, soaked it all in. He was just a fourteen-year-old kid at the time, somehow keeping up with the world's best, failing to wither as the spotlight shined ever brighter. It amazes me now, how we didn't crumble under the pressure of playing in front of a national audience. We weren't out there playing for our own recognition or a paycheck like so many of the pros we had met during that unforgettable week. No, we were playing for our mother.

The one thing she wanted to do, the only thing she wished to see before she died, was to watch her boys play golf. Unlike Brian and me, my older brother, Colton, had never played golf. He was a football player at heart. The sight of watching him get pounded by linebackers made our mother cringe.

She would open her eyes when my dad told her that Colton had safely slipped past the defense and had a clear shot into the end zone. Only then would she open her eyes, flooded with relief, simply glad that her son survived one more play.

When she watched Brian and me play golf, she swelled with a sense of pride. Her two baby boys had received an exemption to play in the Coca Cola Classic at Olympiad and she became a woman reborn. She became her old, healthy self that week, just watching her boys play golf.

In those six days at Olympiad, we captured the heart of a nation. I could see my first putt now as I made my way to the green on No.1. I closed my eyes and the memories flooded through—members of the crowd grabbing my shirt, telling me that I had given them hope, a reason to believe in God and the goodness in people again; how nauseatingly nervous I was as I read the line for my first putt, that 30-footer for birdie.

What, 17 year old kid could ever start a professional golf tournament with a birdie? I had thought that day.

I remembered the crowd. Even on the first day, the grandstands were packed with people eager to see the two brothers from a farm-town on the opposite coast come play so their mother could see them on the course one last time. As my putt slipped just two inches too low, they had let out a collective groan, but followed it with an earsplitting round of applause after I tapped in my par putt. It was as if I had won the whole thing.

In a way, I did.

I chuckled as I thought back to that first hole. For how much flack the American public gets for their demand for drama and gossip. They eat up a heartwarming story like ours. I could never and will never be able to thank them enough for what they did for our family.

After the tournament, when I was safely back in my home in Maryland, our mailbox overflowed with what must have been 40,000 letters thanking Brian and me for our inspiration. It had been our goal to respond to every one of them. Some of the letters were simple, thanking us for reminding them what is most important in life. Some of them were detailed, saying how one of their family members had been diagnosed with cancer and they found our story as a source of inspiration. They became devoted to doing something special, something unforgettable for their own loved ones, because of what we had done.

We were their inspiration.

As I crossed a hidden pathway through a group of palm trees connecting the first green to the 18th tee, I couldn't help thinking back again—back to the day it all began, exactly thirty-four years, to the day. Back to our little town in Parkstead, in what seemed a meaningless golf match against a terrible high school.

CHAPTER 1

God, I loved that ball flight. I loved everything about it.

My ~~pearly~~ white Titleist breezed just along the tree line, teasing the branches that had gotten so much satisfaction from stealing an ~~untold~~ amount of perfect drives all season, and sailed by them, curving back into the fairway with a little draw.

It dropped safely into the short, apple-green grass about 280 yards from the tee box, rocketed off the sun-dried ground and bounded another ten to fifteen feet or so, leaving me with an easy wedge into the green.

It may have been just the first hole but we all knew this was going to be a low round for me today. When I had that ball flight working, there were few in Maryland who could beat me. Call me ~~boastful~~ or bigheaded but it's true. So, I guess you could just call me honest.

I could bend shots around trees at such a sharp angle the ball would look like a piece of paper being ripped by the wind. I could send them sailing over oaks sixty feet high that were just 10 yards in front of me. I could punch them under hungry limbs looking to eat up any unfortunate ball, coming their way only to have it whistle right under their branches and take a sharp hop and stop on a dime a few feet from the pin.

But, of course, golf is a ~~masochistic~~ game meant for the miserable and the insane. It was very rare for me to have this complete control of the ball but I had become so used to playing such ~~erratic~~, risky, give-me-an-eagle-or-a-10 type of golf, I couldn't go back to the safe, take-a-bogey-if-you-have-to type of golf I had been raised to play.

Since I had hit my growth spurt midway through my junior year of high school and ~~sprouted~~ about eight inches overnight, I could hit it farther than two decent players combined. I loved that. There was nothing better than taking out a driver and blasting it over trees to cut a dog leg down by a hundred yards. The only problem, and a rather big one at that, was with the 300-plus yard length I had off the tee and with the rather abstractly artistic element, I sometimes unnecessarily added to my shots, I was about as consistent as a center in basketball shooting free throws.

My younger brother, Brian, who had just teed up his ball, was three years my junior and a shorter, stockier version of me and, befitting our disparate body types, was a much different type of golfer. We could both hit it a mile but he couldn't make a putt if the cup had Bugs Bunny sitting under the hole with a giant magnet, as in Space Jam (one of the all-time greats, mind you). But the kid was an artist with a wedge in his hand. He could open up the face until it was nearly 90 degrees lofted and still have the confidence to take a full swing, sky it 30 feet in the air just to have it come down five feet in front of him purely for the show of it. We always had to one-up each other—much the way brothers do—me with my crafty ball flights and gargantuan drives and him with his deft wedge-work.

No matter how many issues we could potentially have on the course with our rather interesting, homegrown style of play, if we were paired together, we were a hellish tandem to beat.

Just three matches into the fall season, the local papers had already dubbed us the best duo the county had ever seen, possibly even the state. Neither of us really cared for that sort of thing. We were just out there because we loved the game and, of course, because we were driven mad to beat each other.

Our dad had to separate us about a dozen times a round when we were younger. We constantly argued and bickered, claiming the other had somehow cheated to lower his score by the one stroke, typically the difference between us.

Of course, we both knew neither of us would ever cheat with our father around, or even without him around. He was a stern man yet as loving as any father could be. He taught us the difference between playing and playing the right way.

Fathers have a tendency to do that.

"Golf," he always said, his deep blue eyes finding ours no matter how hard we tried to avoid them, "is a gentleman's game—a game of honor and you are going to treat it as such. Do you hear me?"

Even as I walked down the fairway now, with him nowhere in sight, I could hear him in my head as clearly as I had the millions of times I had heard it before. Meanwhile, Brian was busy muttering things to himself in a language only he could understand. His ball hadn't been quite as fortunate as mine. He played it a little too close to the tree line and his ball had caught a stray branch and wound up somewhere in the woods next to the left side of the fairway, a place each of us had been roughly 1,000 times before.

I think I heard him mutter "typical" and "lucky", which probably were good guesses, considering those were his usual go-to lines when I hit a better shot than he did; but nobody will ever know what he said to himself on the course, maybe not even him.

The two poor kids we were playing against were from Ronald Reagan High School just a few miles down the road and, for lack of a better word or explanation, they sucked. Their game was about as pretty as their brown and black uniforms. Reagan had always gotten the short end of the stick when it came to golf just the same as we had always gotten that same treatment with football. I'm actually not too sure why these kids weren't on the football team. They were both built like linebackers—broad shoulders, tree trunks for legs, a neck thick as a keg and arms that seriously tested the elasticity of their shirts. I'm not sure what they fed the kids over there at Reagan. Somehow, every year, they were built like trucks, yet equipped with blistering speed. This subsequently earned them the nickname 'Ronald Roids High.'

My dad, a quarterback in his high school days who had gone on to play a few years in college, always joked he wished we'd moved to Reagan's district where we would have likely ended up playing football. Well, that and because Ronald Reagan was his favorite president. He still has Ronald Reagan pictures hanging in our basement.

Unfortunate for him, or fortunate considering I was about as built for football as the Monstars were for basketball before they stole the NBA players' talents. We had been raised in Parkstead where we grew up in a town that lived and breathed by the health of the local golf course.

That's where we were now, good old Everdeen Hills.

Here I stood, smack dab in the middle of the fairway, completely alone as Brian crashed through the woods looking for his ball.

He had turned one of his irons into a makeshift machete, whipping it into as many unlucky branches as possible, where having a chainsaw in his bag might just have been worth it. The Reagan kids were somewhere off to the right in the neighboring ninth fairway, which ran parallel to the first hole but in the reverse direction. I chuckled as they moved farther and farther away from our hole and closer to the ninth tee box.

Football players, indeed.

I turned and focused on my upcoming shot, nothing more than an easy sand wedge. The blue flag on top of the pin meant it was in the back, just over the second-tier of the green that stretched about 60-feet deep. *Leave it short and it's almost a sure three-putt. Sling it over and I'll be left with a nasty chip that would give the best players in the world cold sweats.* I only had about 100 yards left to the back so I pulled out my sand wedge.

A gap wedge would go way over and a full-swing lob wedge was too stupid for even reckless me to try. I glanced around to see if anybody else was ready to take his shot. Nobody was, so I stepped up to my ball.

The setting sun put a devilish glare even on the wedge's graphite-colored clubface. I turned my focus away from the club and onto a target just in front of the ball, a nifty trick my dad had taught me when I was ten.

It took only a three-quarter, watery-smooth swing and as soon as I hit it, I knew it was going to be good. One of the greatest feelings in the world is a purely hit golf ball. It's almost as if you hit nothing at all, completely effortless. That's exactly what it felt like now. A wallet-sized divot flew from the ground as my ball took off, high and straight at the pin and into the merciless sun.

I lost sight of it moments after impact but I really didn't have to look to know it was going to be good. My mother clapped as I heard the soft thud of my ball hitting the green. I didn't know if it had made it to the second tier or not and there was no way my mom could have either. However, regardless of the result, she would cheer just the same.

She was an incredible woman, my mother. Somehow she balanced the duties of raising three children—all boys, no less—playing the role of cook, chauffeur, maid and devoted fan among at least a dozen other things. She managed to make it to every single one of my older brother Colton's football games, even though she couldn't bear watching him take a handoff.

She would squeeze my dad's arm, wince when she heard the sound of pads crashing together, and then peek out with one eye, as a child plays hide and seek, only to see that about 99 percent of the time Colton was nowhere near the scrum in the middle of the field. He would be darting outside the fray, flitting this way and that, making a mockery of nearly every unfortunate defender who made any attempt to bring him down.

Poor Colt, ending up at Parkstead High with us. It was a black hole for football players. Even with his heart-stopping speed and remarkable ability to run 40 yards just to gain three, he had no chance with the puny offensive line that Parkstead threw in front of him. Still, he had had his cleats, jitterbug moves and an indomitable spirit, which earned him a scholarship to a little Division-III school to play running back, a much different future from his two younger brothers who had never known the blood sweat and tears attitude of a football field. We preferred the etiquette and quiet serenity of a golf course.

Well, I preferred that quiet serenity, at least. I was typically calmer than Brian, who had finally found his ball in the middle of the forest. It appeared to be buried under a collage of brightly colored early-fall leaves. The Reagan kids had found theirs in the other fairway, albeit the wrong one but a fairway, none-the-less.

I saw the glimmer of one of Brian's irons, as he hacked his ball out of the woods. It thwacked one tree and zipped into another but somehow pin-balled its way out of the blanket of leaves and into the rough where it came to rest about the same distance from the hole where my drive had landed.

I still hadn't even moved after I had hit my ball, still had no idea if it was going to be an easy birdie putt, an impossible 2-putt or a heart-attack-inducing downhill chip. As calm a person as my mother had raised me to be, I was already getting frustrated.

I hated slow play, just like my father. As much as I hate to admit it, I was just a seventeen-year-old version of my father, Don Lammey. The way he felt about things like slow play, I felt the same.

In what seemed like an eternity, which, realistically, was probably a maximum of five minutes, I watched the Reagan kids roll, shank, duff and scoot their ball ten more times before they reached the green. It made me wince watching them. They reminded me a bit of Crabbe and Goyle in Harry Potter. I hated playing with bad golfers.

To my relief, Brian had finally emerged from the woods, covered in sweat and dirt with a few leaves tangled in his shaggy brown hair.

He got to his ball and didn't even take a practice swing. He just stepped up and ripped at it and, even in the thick Everdeen Hills rough, he was able to knock it to what appeared to be on the second tier with me.

He slipped the club back into his bag without wiping it down and threw the bag over his shoulder. We walked to the green in silence until he let out a low whistle when he saw our balls sitting side by side about five feet from the pin.

"Ten says I'm closer," he said, flashing a cocky grin, a grin that should never be allowed on a freshman's face.

Despite my frustration with the glacial pace of the round induced by the Reagan kids, I felt a smile creeping. Competition, especially with Brian, put a fire in my belly every single time. I could forget about the Reagan kids.

"I tell you what," I said. "I'll bet you I'm closer, and I'll even spot you three strokes the rest of the round. Winner does the trash tonight and dishes tomorrow."

Our only two chores—the trash and the dishes. We didn't even have to feed Jake, our yellow lab, or take him out when he needed to go about his business. Our parents asked very little of us and we still barely managed to do the only two things they did ask us to do. But I knew if one of us had to do it because of a lost bet, the other would never let him forget about it.

"Oh, you're on, big brudda," he said, extending a hand and then pulling it away as I went to shake it, acting like he was slicking back his hair.

Typical freshman, I thought but I was still unable to keep from laughing a little at his antics.

When we got to the green, it turned out his was, in fact, closer, by maybe an inch. Nevertheless, to him, an inch may as well have been a foot, a yard, 100 miles.

"Told ya."

"I'm so nervous. I mean, you're such a good putter," I said, sarcasm dripping from my mouth. "Actually, why don't you just pick it up now since we all know it's automatic anyway, right?"

"You're still a-wayyy," he sang.

I smiled. I loved it.

I crouched down low, about three feet behind my ball, to read the putt, my knees cracking enough to sound like somebody just dropped a couple drumsticks on the ground (growing pains). I'd had this little 5-foot putt about a million times. It would slide a little to the left, maybe an inch, if I had the right speed. The greens looked as if they'd just been rolled that morning, which meant the ball would probably run a little quicker than normal.

As soon as I hit it, I knew it was in. I didn't even watch it as it rolled towards the cup. Brian knew, too.

I saw him look my direction. I winked and blew him a kiss.

"You take any notes, sweetheart?" I crooned as the ball hit the bottom of the cup, making a satisfying 'dink' as it did.

"Even a broken clock is right twice a day," he grumbled.

My mother, of course, reacted as if I had just won the U.S. Open.

"Way to go, Jay," she exclaimed. "Woo."

Brian's putt dropped halfway down on the right side of the cup, took a 360-degree turn and popped out. He proceeded to tomahawk his putter into the ground, spraying dirt and grass all over and let out a string of curses that would make a sailor blush.

"Well, I guess you should have taken notes," I said, laughing as I slipped my putter back into my bag.

Much to my pleasure and my little brother's displeasure, that was generally how the rest of the round went.

My swing was just as silky as it had been on the first two shots. I don't think I missed a fairway or green all day. Brian kept challenging me double or nothing as I rolled in birdie after birdie—five, in all. He didn't play badly, tapping in for par on the ninth hole to shoot a 1-over-par 37. But very few high school players would have been able to get within three shots of my five-under 31, which somebody, I forget who, told me broke some age-old county record.

After I picked my ball out of the ninth hole, I pointed directly to Brian.

"Trash tonight, dishes tomorrow…freshman."

That always got him going. He hated being ridiculed for being the youngest. He didn't even bother shaking Crabbe and Goyle's hands afterwards, storming off and throwing his bag over his shoulder as he went.

Before I could even get off the green, my mother was wrapping me up in a bone-crunching hug.

"Oh my god, oh my god, oh my god, you were wonderful," she shouted.

My cheeks burned with embarrassment. I tried to nudge her away just a little bit so I could get off the green. The group behind us still had to make their approach shots.

My coach, Mr. Hamilton, thumped me on my back as I made my way off the backside of the green, toward the cart path.

"I see Brian's lost some sort of bet," he laughed, pointing at Brian, who was already waiting by my clunky little Honda Civic.

"Something like that," I chuckled.

I was about halfway to the parking lot before another person, someone I had never seen before, or at least I thought I hadn't, but he did look awfully familiar, called me over.

"Young man," he said, leaning his enormous frame against a pine tree next to the driving range. It seemed to bow a little under his weight. "You have one more minute?"

I sighed, held up a finger to Brian to let him know I would just be a minute, and made my way over to the man.

He had to be one of the largest people I'd ever seen. He was at least 300 pounds and had more chins than any normal person should have. Nevertheless, he had a friendly face and a Santa Clause-like twinkle in his brilliant blue eyes.

"Name's Mike," he said, extending a chubby, sweaty hand. "Mike Oberdorf. That was a hell of a round you had there, son."

The name rung so many bells in my head but I couldn't place it. I'd google it later.

I took his hand and tried to shake it but it ended up being more like a slippery high five.

"Thanks. I'm Jay. I guess I hit it alright out there," I said sheepishly.

I was never any good at accepting praise.

"Alright?" he exclaimed. "Son, I've seen alright. I've seen good. I've seen remarkable. What you did out there was flat out stupid good but I'm not here to talk about your round. I'm here to talk to you about where you're playing golf next year because, son, I'd damn well like you to be playing for me."

CHAPTER 2

"Who was that?" snorted Brian, as I climbed into my little beat-up Civic.

I could hardly talk my smile was so big. My cheeks had actually started to hurt.

"He was uh...he was," I couldn't get through it. I was giggling with excitement. "You'll see."

However, as we drove home, I still couldn't place where I had heard that name before or why he looked so familiar. At the moment, I was too giddy to care.

I had been recruited before, but never in person. Coaches would always get turned off by my glaring inconsistencies. They would call me after I would fire a 67 in some tournament but then a week later tell me they would be "pursuing other options," when I followed it up with a spectacularly atrocious 92.

The few who had expressed real interest in me were from smaller schools. They knew I could go as low as any high school kid in the country could and I could probably draw some serious attention for it. Nevertheless, even they had their hesitations about extending any sort of scholarship offer. I was one of the riskiest moves a coach could make. Maybe I would somehow find a consistent swing and keep the majority of my rounds at par or better but there was an equally good chance my swing would disappear altogether and I would make the coach look like an idiot for wasting a scholarship.

I had never really minded what little attention I did get. I knew I could play and I knew there were certain days where it looked like it might have been my first time ever touching a club. I knew I was putting coaches in a tough spot and realized I might not get the offer that would likely be extended to Brian in a few years.

Brian had been playing since he could pick up a twig. He had never felt the lure of a basketball court or the glorious temptation of becoming a football star like Colton. Golf had been his one and only love. His swing came as naturally and reliably as the sunrise. He never had days where he would shoot 92 or 97, as I so regularly did. He would stomp and snort and throw fits anytime he was over par, even if it was just one-over like today.

Me? I was just thankful to walk off the course with a ball left in my bag.

He didn't speak the whole ride home. He just stared out the window, pondering the "what-ifs" that every golfer, no matter the handicap, will go through after each round.

What if I hadn't hit that drive out of bounds on No. 3? What if I'd run in that 12-footer on five or chipped in that easy look on six? What if, what if, what if?

He was especially caught up in them this time because I had beaten him. Well, "beaten him" doesn't quite describe it. I crushed, clobbered, destroyed and, most of all embarrassed him. Even if I was three years his senior, he couldn't stand losing, especially to anybody who shared the same blood as him.

The five-minute commute home wasn't enough time for him to give his round a full examination. As he did after most of his bad rounds, he remained in the passenger seat as I got out.

I had only opened the squeaky screen door to my house before my mother was wrapping me in a hug again.

"Congratulations." she exclaimed. "You were awesome. Where's Brian? Pouting in the car again? Who was that man you talked to after the round? What did he want? Was he a college recruiter? Where is he from?"

"Whoa, easy there. Settle down for a second," I said, freeing myself from her grasp while trying to soak in the barrage of questions.

"First, thanks. I played pretty well, I guess."

"You sure di…" she said, trying to interrupt before I put a finger up to stop her.

"Let me finish," I said, exhaling.

"Yes, Brian is in the car thinking about how badly I just kicked his ass. That man was a college recruiter from Alcorn…"

This time, there was no stopping her. Her normally deep brown eyes lit up like the Griswold's house in Christmas Vacation (another one of my all-time favorites).

"Alcorn? Alcorn? Honey, that's amazing. Congratulations!.

She hugged me again.

"Mom, c'mon. I get it, it's a big deal. He's actually coming over right now for dinner."

I was immediately freed from her grasp.

"Right now?" she squealed.

She hurried into the kitchen to tidy up. I made my way to the family room but I could still hear her talking to herself a million miles an hour.

"Alcorn....I wonder what he's like. Does he like chicken? I hope he likes chicken because that's what we're having. Well from the looks of him, he'll eat just about anything. Ah, but this place is so dirty. I have to clean, I have to…"

I clicked on the TV and let the sounds of SportsCenter drown out her incessant muttering. Finally, a moment to enjoy my round all by myself. Well, almost. Jake came trotting in and flopped down next to me on our black, leather couch. A few seconds later, Brian came thundering through the house, slamming every unlucky door in his way.

Yeah, some moment.

"What's for dinner?" I heard him ask my poor mother, who was already freaking out about Mr. Oberdorf's coming over.

"It's your favorite, Brian's chicken," she hastily replied.

Brian simply grunted his approval and belly-flopped onto the couch next to me.

28

"You should be nicer to her, you know," I said.

"Oh shut up, pretty boy. We can't all be Mr. California like you. Shit, if I'd played like you half the time I'd have already quit golf and picked up badminton or something girlish like that. You'd be good at something like that."

"You're right, I guess waxing you by six shots in nine holes just wasn't good enough. Or getting recruited by Alcorn isn't very good either."

That shut him up.

His dream was to go to Alcorn like our father. The college had won two national championships in golf each of the last two years. The idea of hoisting an NCAA trophy was something we both knew he could not live without.

"Is that who that person was?" he asked. The tone of his voice had gone from anger to something that resembled a humbled awe.

"Yep. Should be here any minute, actually."

He shot up off the couch, sprinted over to the window and peeked out through our red curtains.

"Shit. Is that him walking up right now? Ughhh, he watched me shoot a 37. A 37."

"Oh shut up. You act like that's bad. Try shooting a 97 after having three coaches call you the week before."

He sniggered and ran over to the door, eager to meet Mr. Oberdorf. I heard Brian open the door and stammer out some form of hello before the two made their way into the kitchen.

Whatever my mother was cooking smelled awesome. She had laid out a tray of shredded chicken marinated in barbeque sauce, a pile of French fries, fruit salad, and some kind of strawberry jello thing topped with whipped cream. I don't know exactly what it was, but I certainly wasn't asking any questions.

By the time we had all taken our seats, Mr. Oberdorf had already wolfed down half his food. There was something I liked about the man but I couldn't quite pin it down. Maybe it was the fact he was so homegrown and not uber-professional as many recruiters would be. Most of them barely touched the food when they came to see Colton, only eating it because it would be rude not to eat. Not Oberdorf—this man from Alcorn, the most prestigious college golf program in the country, just put his head down and went for it. Maybe that meant he wasn't all that serious about recruiting me, which I honestly expected and could live with. Or, maybe this was just who he was, putting it all out there for everyone to see.

"So, Mr. Oberdorf, is it?" my mother asked.

"Yes ma'am. You got it. On the first try too, not many people do. Most people will go with O-Bee-Darf or O-Beer-Dorf, something like that."

"And you're interested in Jay playing golf for you?"

"Well, interested I don't think quite describes it. This boy," he said, pointing a grubby, barbeque stained finger at me, "is truly something special. I've never seen a high-schooler work the ball like him in all my years in this business and, let me tell you something, it's been quite a few."

I could feel my face turning bright red. Brian, who had been so excited to meet him, was clearly getting frustrated with me getting all the fame, at the moment.

"If it were up to me," Oberdorf continued. "I'd offer him a full-boat right now. Unfortunately, we have to do all this formal, important stuff like filling out papers and documents nobody looks at or cares about, to be honest. Then it has to be approved by somebody in some office, who then tells me if it's a go or not. But, like I said, I've never seen a talent like him, except for maybe that little man seated across from him."

This time he pointed to Brian, who immediately perked up.

"You're saying awfully nice things," said my mother, beaming at the two of us. "I don't know what to say."

"Well," he said, rising out of his chair and bringing his plate over to the sink. "I tell you what. If these boys, Jay in particular, can keep this type of play up. You don't have to say much. Their game is going to be doing plenty of talking for all three of ya."

He rinsed off his dishes, slipped them into the washer and turned to leave.

"Here's my card," he said, passing me a little blue business card with the golden Alcorn Ram logo shining up at me. "Call me anytime you'd like, whether it be that you just want to chat or you get the case of the shanks."

He paused and winked at me. He must have known my unfortunate proclivity for those cursed shanks, sometimes.

"Or if you want to tell me that you smoked your brother again. Either way, I'll keep in touch. It was wonderful meeting y'all, I can't thank you enough for that delicious dinner, but it's about time for me to be getting back home."

With that, he waddled out, leaving the three of us all stoplight red from his radiant praise.

"What a pleasant man he is," my mother gasped after a few minutes. "I'm so proud of you boys."

After dinner, I helped my mother clean up and tidy the kitchen. When I went up to my room to shower and relax, Brian stood in the hallway with a smirk, clutching a bottle of something clear but, judging from the look on his face, it certainly wasn't water.

"I think even a pretty boy like you, knows what this calls for," he said, waggling the bottle in front of me. "It's time to celebrate."

CHAPTER 3

The bass blasting from the house 50 yards away sent vibrations through my little Civic as I pulled up to Mike Cheyene's driveway.

The kid was crazy. Always throwing parties, always doing the craziest shit you could imagine—skydiving, picking fights, motorcycle races. He was that kid with the fake ID that every high school seems to have. Anytime somebody needed alcohol, Mikey was your man.

An adrenaline junkie at heart, the kid was out of his mind. Nevertheless, everybody loved him. Even the parents who knew of his less than responsible lifestyle adored him. He was charming and fun, always saying please and thank you, but then never failing to throw back 10 shots and do a backflip into his pool off his roof—*his roof.*

Somehow, he never, and I mean never, got caught. The cops made routine visits to his house but he was so good at hiding what was going on he never got hit with anything more than a warning. His four-story mansion was tucked back beyond Beckerstreet road, deep in the woods, protected by massive pine trees in the front and an endless forest in the back. No matter how loud he blasted his music—which he took full advantage of—nobody who wasn't invited would even hear a blip.

Everybody in the school knew Mikey, even Brian, a freshman. The kid had a reputation for throwing the craziest bangers of the year, ranging from toga parties to beer Olympics that attracted anybody who was anybody at Parkstead High. Naturally, this one was no different.

As Brian and I walked down the pine needle covered path to his house, we could hear the chants of some attention-starved kid going on his 30th second in a keg stand.

"31, 32, 33," bellowed a rowdy crowd, clearly in a drunken stupor even though it wasn't even midnight yet.

"You're lucky you shot so low today," Brian said.

"And why is that?"

"Well, you're gonna have to do a keg stand for every stroke. That's how it works."

Of course, my freshman baby brother would be telling me "how it works" in the drinking world.

"Double or nothing says I beat you again," I said, punching him in the arm hard enough for him to drop the case of cheap piss-water beer he was hauling.

"Freshman," I added, flashing a cocky grin back at him as I turned and quickened my pace to the party, growing louder with every step I took.

I turned the corner and hopped onto Mikey's deck and was greeted by a roar from the belligerent crowd.

"Jay, Jay, Jay, Jay," they slurred, half in unison, half trailing off on their own pace.

"Keg-stand, Keg-stand," began another chant from somewhere on the balcony, two stories above.

Christ, I'd only been here two seconds and I was already getting pushed into doing a keg stand.

"Can somebody toss me a b…" I began to ask but was cut off. Somebody behind me had grabbed my feet and was hoisting me upside down into the air. Whoever was holding my legs, were doing a bad job of it. They stumbled forward, knocking my head into a pair of knees and shins, hauling me toward the keg.

"Jay, Jay, Jay," began the crowd again. I rolled my eyes, hoisted myself on top of the keg with my left arm, grabbed the nozzle with my right, and went for it.

Forty five seconds later I was lying on the soaking wet pool deck, lightheaded, close to vomiting and giggling my ass off.

"You ssseee that?" I coughed at Brian, who had a beer in each hand. "45 seconds, 45 freakin' seconds,"

"Oh, yea, you must be so proud, out-drinking your freshman brother for a whole forty-five seconds," he replied sarcastically. "You're a real heavyweight, let me tell you."

I tried to get up but my head did about a 400 degree turn and, before I knew it, I was back on the refreshingly cold pool deck.

"Gimme a minute. I'll be up at it in a sec."

I just lay there, waiting for the spins to die out while the rest of the party raged on. After a few minutes, I was back up again, wading through the shirtless and bikini-clad crowd while being offered drinks and shots everywhere I went. Some of the shots were fruity. Some were bitter. Some burned. Some cooled. I knew I'd feel every single one of them in a few minutes. After about half an hour of fighting through the mob of teenagers, I finally plowed my way inside to the unfinished basement and worked my way onto the beer pong table with Brian.

"You see your girl yet?" he asked, grinning.

"What? Who?"

I clutched to the table to keep my balance. The shots were beginning to take their toll. My vision was getting a little blurry. My legs didn't seem to be working quite right.

"Oh c'mon don't play dumb with me. Morgan's here and you know it."

"She is?"

I tried to stand up straight but immediately thought better of it, grabbing back onto the table.

Brian roared with laughter.

"Oh, yea, that looks believable."

I let go of the table and tried to stand on my own but again failed. To make matters worse, a pair of hands covered up my eyes.

"Guess who?" whispered an all-too familiar voice.

My heartbeat must have tripled in a second. I loved that voice.

I grinned, resisting the urge to turn around and wrap Morgan up in what would likely be a falling, stumbling, sloppy hug.

"Hmm, I don't know. Alex?"

"Nope, guess again."

I could feel her warm breath against my ear. She smelled of watermelon and vodka. I spluttered a little bit and tried to regain my cool. She was too good at this.

"Umm...uhh, Catie?" I asked, making my best attempt at playing it off.

"God, you're cute," she said, uncovering my eyes and spinning me around. Before I could even get a grip of my surroundings again, her fingers were running through my hair and she pulled her body tightly against mine and gave me a long, wet kiss. I think my heart exploded right there.

"Uhh, big bro," cut in Brian. "We're trying to play a game here. Either get a room so I can get a new partner or put your little lady down and shoot."

My face must have been stoplight red. I turned back towards the table but couldn't stop smiling. My cheeks actually hurt...again.

"You mind if I play this one?" I turned and asked Morgan, who was leaning her head on my shoulder, her impossibly blonde hair spilling down her back.

"Do your thing, Jay," she said, slapping me on the butt. "I'll just be outside in my little. Tiny. Itty. Bitty. Bikini."

She spun and headed towards the deck, slipping off her shirt in the process to show a bikini top of which her mother certainly would not have approved.

For a minute, we all just stared, watching her strut out of the room.

"You sure you would rather play beer pong with three other dudes than go be with that?" laughed Brian. "I tell you what, I'm not letting you play. Please, for the love of God, go be thankful a girl so hot could ever possibly consider you."

He didn't have to say it twice. I tossed the ping pong ball behind my head and practically ran. Well, I did a drunken version of running, to catch up to her.

"That took you longer than I thought," she said, when I got to her. She turned around and grabbed my hands, pulling me in close again.

"You want to get a little wet?"

Her nose was touching mine and I could feel her hands sliding down my torso until they gripped my waistband. She pulled me in a little closer.

"I think you should come get wet with me."

Any cool that I had, which wasn't much, before was completely gone. Obliterated, incinerated, vanished, gone; whatever you want to call it, I had none of it.

"I..uhh…err…um..you look…wow," was all I managed.

"You're too cute, Jay," she giggled, turning and taking a few steps toward the pool. "Get that shirt off and come swim with me."

My shirt was on the deck in a matter of seconds. She shimmied out of her skirt to reveal an equally tiny bikini bottom. I breathed hard and shook my head. Brian was right. I was way out of my league here.

I slipped into the pool after her as she drifted back towards the deep end that was dimly lit and away from the fray of the throngs of yelling, obnoxious drunks.

"Well, what do we do now?" I asked, finally regaining a little bit of my cool as the drunkenness turned from sloppy to overconfident.

"Just be quiet and kiss me."

Her fingers were working their way through my hair again, pulling my face into hers. I floated in as close as I could, my hands running down her Goosebumps-riddled body, which might as well have been naked considering how tiny the American flag bathing suit was that she was wearing.

"Jay," she breathed, moving down and kissing my neck. "Let's go upstairs, or to your car. Let's get out of here."

My mind blanked on what to say. This girl, widely considered as one of the best looking in the school, was asking, no, suggesting, I take her to my bedroom or car.

"Car it is," I whispered into her ear.

We snagged our clothes and raced across the wet yard, falling and stumbling the whole way, with her holding my hand and giggling behind me.

"This is crazy," she laughed. "Are we actually doing this?"

"Your idea," I called back.

I fumbled with my keys, desperately trying to open the damn Civic. What was I even bothering with the keys for? The passenger door hadn't been able to lock for years. I ripped it open, slid the seat all the way up to the front and helped Morgan slip into the back. I clambered in and checked to make sure nobody was spying before I closed the door behind me.

My 6-foot-4 frame was not an ideal fit for a little backseat hookup but Lord was I going to do everything in my power to make it work. We laughed and giggled and stripped, banging against the roof and door and bumping into each other every two seconds.

"You're fun," she giggled. "I didn't think you would actually do something like this."

"Well, you never know what a 45-second keg stand followed with about 100 shots will make you do," I said, giving her a swift kiss.

My legs were jammed against the door in the most awkward angle of all time and I knew I was squishing her. She was only about 100 pounds soaking wet and I had all 190 or so pounds of me lying directly on top of her. I looked down at her and we both started bursting into laughter.

"This will never work," she said in between a fit of giggles.

"I should have picked the bedroom."

I punched the driver's seat mock anger.

We untangled ourselves in a half-naked mess. I sat up, kissed Morgan on the cheek, and began slipping my button down shirt back on when I saw a sight that made my heart stop.

I couldn't believe it. This couldn't happen. Not now. Not today. Not on the day I had received an unofficial college scholarship offer. But it was happening anyway. Right in front of me.

Blue and red lights, hordes of them, flashed about a hundred yards down the road, flying right for the driveway.

CHAPTER 4

My heart sank faster than a brick in a kiddie pool. I froze, staring absentmindedly at the dizzying army of flashing lights booking it towards our direction. I could hear Morgan screaming something but I was too far off in my own little world to make out what she was saying. It sounded she was trying to talk to me underwater, the noises were audible but entirely unclear and distant.

Really? I thought. *This would be the one freaking time Mikey gets caught. The line of cars dotting Beckerstreet must have given us away. A passing patrol car, familiar with Mikey's habit for testing the rules, probably called it in, figures.*

"Brian," I finally said, snapping out of my daze. The cars were about 50 yards away now and closing in fast. There must have been five or six of them.

"Brian. We gotta get him out of there."

I turned to look at Morgan, who was somehow already fully dressed, her hands flying around her phone's keyboard, dialing up my brother. I threw my clothes back on, watching her out of the corner of my eye. She bit her lip nervously, as the rings continued.

"Dammit," she hissed, slamming the flip phone shut. "Let's go then."

We fell out the passenger door and stumbled down the driveway.

"Hold it right there," demanded a deep voice through a megaphone behind us. "This is the police."

We ignored it and ran on, hand-in-hand, completely ignoring the cop. We could hear the sounds of several footsteps now chasing after us and the beams of the flashlights kept passing over us, illuminating the stray trees, into which we very nearly barreled.

Morgan pulled out her phone again and dialed Brian in one final, desperate attempt to get him out of the house. She had barely put the little flip phone to her ear before suddenly veering off into the woods on the right.

"Brian, get your ass out of there right now," she hissed. "There are shit tons of cops coming. They will be there in like, 30 seconds. Use the cellar door. That's your best bet. Make it quick and don't bring anybody."

"Genius, Morgs," I said, kissing her on the cheek, as we slipped deeper into the woods where the cellar door was. They would never check there.

Hardly anybody knew Mikey even had a cellar door, let alone the cops.

We hadn't been followed around to the back of the house. The police had barged right in through the front, not even bothering to knock. Morgan and I walked through the woods, treading softly, trying to make the least amount of noise possible, so as not to attract the attention of any stray cop, wandering around to make sure there was nobody escaping a citation. The adrenaline rush still had me shaking and I was still mighty buzzed. I began giggling for no real reason as we tip-toed through the trees. The moonlight caused our shadows to dance playfully in front of us as we went.

"I swear to god, if your little shit of a brother doesn't come and we get in trouble I'm going to kill you," she said, trying to give me a glare but unable to keep the corners of her mouth from curling back into a grin. Moments like these, as incredibly stressful as they were, were also such a god-damn blast.

"Oh c'mon, even you can't say this hasn't been fun, little miss perfect."

"I'm little miss perfect now? Is that what you tell your friends my name is?" she asked, pulling me in again so her mouth was right against mine.

"'Cause I know you talk about me. All The Time."

There it was again. My heartbeat going off like a damn racehorse. I tried not to breath heavy but it was no good. I gave in.

"Dammit, Morgs. You're too good at this."

I kissed her and she wrapped her arms around my neck and pressed her body up against mine. Things were getting rolling again and then BANG.

"Whoaaa," crooned Brian as he crawled out of the cellar. "What do we have going on here?"

Even in the dim moonlight, I could see Morgan blushing. She put her head down so I wouldn't see but she was practically glowing red.

"You're lucky we warned you, you little shit," I laughed. "Let's get out of here."

"Wellllll, that might not be so easy, big bro. You see," he said.

He motioned his arm towards the cellar.

"I brought my people here with me on this here underground railroad."

And just like that, dozens of bodies materialized from the cellar, pouring out into the woods. For the second time of the night, my heart sank. There was no way we were going to make it out of here with all these people. Our only chance would be to make a break for it and run, but I knew Brian wouldn't just leave all of his friends and let them get scooped up.

"What are we supposed to do with all of them?"

"I don't know, couldn't just leave 'em, man. That would be effed up."

"Morgs? Any brilliant ideas?"

Her embarrassment had apparently turned to anger in a matter of seconds.

"Yea," she replied darkly. "Kill your little brother, that's one."

"Easy sweetheart," replied Brian, putting his hands up in surrender. "Just trying to help my people out, here."

"Quit saying 'my people,'" she snapped. "Jay c'mon, we can't get caught. Especially not you, not tonight, right after you pretty much received a scholarship to Alcorn."

The thought had never even dawned on me. I could lose that offer. Well, it technically wasn't an offer yet but I could lose any chance of going to Alcorn if I got a citation. My heart started pounding again. God that was getting annoying.

"Well shit, she's probably right, bro," muttered Brian. "You gotta go. I'll figure this shit out."

"No, Brian. If I had wanted, I'd already be back home. I wanted to come make sure you got out fine. We're leaving together. Besides, mom would kill me if I left you hanging out to dry. I wouldn't be going to college anyway because I'd be dead."

Finally, we all laughed. The situation we were in was almost comical: cops no more than 30 yards from our hiding spot, certain trouble awaiting, a scholarship begging to be revoked—all after the best round of golf of my life.

"Well, it doesn't look like this choice is up to us anymore, dude," cut in Brian, pointing towards a beam of light pinned on the army of kids he had brought through the cellar.

"Cops found us, let's go people, let's go," he bellowed. "Time to see who the fastest kid in our school is. I got twenty says Tony gets caught, ya fat ass."

Kids scattered like a flock of birds hearing gunfire and soon dozens of flashlight beams began scouring the woods as our herd ran left and right.

"Alright, this way," I said, taking Morgan by the hand and pointing towards the side of the woods that would lead us well behind Mikey's house and take us to the main road in about a mile and so we went, Brian, Morgan and I, crashing through the trees. After about 10 minutes of falling, slipping, falling again and trudging through the woods, we tumbled out into the street in a sweating, panting, bloody, mud-caked mess.

"I think we're good, dude," coughed Brian.

"Yea…we…we should be….we should be OK," Morgan spluttered. She leaned heavily on my chest to keep from falling. "Let's just walk in from here."

We reeked of salt and alcohol and looked like a bunch of homeless kids. Brian's shaggy brown hair had leaves strewn all over it, his arms were cut and bloodied, his face was lined with streaks of dirt and sweat. Morgan's pink tank top had turned a soft shade of red; her normally tan arms were now even darker with the mud and kicked up leaves and dirt from the woods. I couldn't imagine I looked much better. My once sky-blue button down had rips and holes all over it, my legs stung from the cuts and my eyes burned from the alcoholic sweat, dripping into them.

We limped the half mile or so left to home, looking like three of the most ridiculous kids on the planet. Brian, through all of this, didn't have a care in the world, singing Kenny Chesney's "Never wanted nothing more" as we walked. But my stomach did a flip with every step we took.

We might have escaped the police but there was one thing I feared far more than any cop or school suspension and that was my father.

CHAPTER 5

In seventeen years, I'd never seen my dad like this. His face made a tomato look pale. His brilliant blue eyes gleamed with a rage I'd never seen.

I'd have rather been looking at a rattlesnake.

Don't get me wrong, I had seen my dad mad. The worst had to be the time I broke Brian's arm when we were playing football in our cul-de-sac because he had legitimately roasted me for a touchdown. Naturally, I picked him up and slammed him to the ground as he was doing a touchdown dance. Pops wasn't happy.

However, this was on a new level. He didn't even have the energy to scream. He just paced back and forth in our kitchen, while we shrunk as far down into our chairs as possible. We hadn't even showered or changed yet.

I thought I caught a glimpse of Brian snickering as our dad's face changed from red to purple to blue then cycled through each again before he finally let out a breath. It was really quite terrifying.

My mom waited in the corner next to our cereal cabinet, probably more scared for us than we were. Our father was a disciplinarian. His dad had been in the air force, his brother, my Uncle Matt, had been a Marine and his youngest brother, my Uncle Marcus, had been a Navy SEAL. Any room for error, especially like the doozie Brian and I had pulled tonight, was just flat out unacceptable.

"Are you…" he began before cutting off and running his hand through his bushy mustache. It seemed to twitch with a rage of its own.

He paced back again and gave it another whirl.

"Are you boys out of your god damn minds?"

My dad never cursed. And when I say never, I mean never. The only other time I'd heard a swear word come out of his mouth was when a coach ordered his pitcher to throw a bean ball at me in rec baseball.

"I tell you what, ass hole," he had bellowed into the coach's face. "You try that again, and you got a whole 'nother thing comin'."

Nobody ever tried to hit me with a pitch again.

But tonight, I was that coach. I was that coach to whom he was spewing profanity. Not a good place to be.

"Jay, not three hours after you get a scholarship offer from Alcorn, from Alcorn,"

He was roaring now.

"My alma mater, no less. And you go and pull a stunt like this?"

Now he turned to Brian, who was examining his hands as if they were the most fascinating things he had ever seen.

"And Brian, you're fourteen years old. Fourteen. Do you know how old the drinking age is? Do you know it?"

Our dad crossed his arms over his chest and glowered at us. Sure, I stood 6'4" and was a good four inches taller than him but right now, I think I was a maximum of 4'10".

"Sir, I just want to…" I tried to say but he cut me off before I could finish.

"Did I ask for you to speak?"

He slammed his fist on the table, knocking over the salt and pepper shakers.

"Well, you did ask if I knew how old the drinking age was," Brian courageously and quite stupidly cut in. "He was going to help me with that."

Dad didn't even bother to respond. He just turned his wilting gaze over to him and Brian went back to examining his hands.

"You boys have made me one of the proudest fathers in all of Parkstead for nearly 20 years. You've never given me much reason to come down too hard on you. I've been tough on you because it makes you better men and better people. But tonight…"

He turned his back to us and put his hands behind his head.

"Tonight is the most embarrassed I've ever been. You boys go out drinking, celebrating a worthless win over the most pitiful excuse for a golf team I've ever seen, nearly get arrested, and then show up in my house, looking like a bunch of bums. You're lucky I don't kick the both of you out, right now."

"Donald, I think that's enough," whispered my mother, from her corner.

"Jan, this is not the time," he said, waving her off and returning his stony gaze back to us.

"You," he said, pointing at my chest. "You almost got Morgan arrested."

"Hold it right there," I said, standing up and pointing right back at him.

The anger had finally bubbled out of me. Or maybe I was too drunk to care. Who knows.

"We're the only reason Morgan didn't get arrested. Brian, the only reason half the people there didn't get arrested. You only knew about any of this because you're best friends with Chief Wilkins who said he knew we were friends with Mikey and we might be there. We could have been anywhere. Maybe we were just out playing football and that's why we're all muddy and ragged.

"You assumed the worst, which is frankly ridiculous, considering we haven't gotten so much as an hour of detention in our entire lives combined. We kept about thirty people from getting arrested and getting citations and getting suspended and losing eligibility for the rest of the fall season."

I probably should have stopped there but I was a snowball. And I was rolling down a mountain.

"We did that. Us. Me and Brian. Your sons. Now, I'm well aware we gave you plenty of reason to be mad. We did something we shouldn't have, sure. But we're human teenage boys and I'd say we've done pretty damn well for ourselves so far and I'd say we did pretty damn well for ourselves tonight. I bet Morgan's parents don't have a freakin' clue she was even there. Why? Because we were there to make sure she didn't get in trouble."

I was nose to nose with my dad by the time I finished. From where Brian was sitting, it probably looked like a manager getting in the face of the umpire.

"Well," he said coolly, pushing me roughly back into my seat. "Would you look at that, honey. We raised a bunch of little heroes.

"I tell you what. You boys get yourselves cleaned up because I don't want a bunch of raggedy looking bums in my house anymore. Get to bed and we're going to have a long, long talk in the morning."

I fought back tears with all my might as I tried to match my father's stoic glare. But I couldn't hold it. The tears started to fall and I snapped my head away and headed for the stairs, roughly bumping into his shoulder as I went. I could hear the thud of Brian's footsteps following mine as I raced up to my room.

"Whoa, look at big bro getting big on pops," he said, slipping into my room and quietly shutting it closed. "I see you. Way to hold it down in there."

He tried to offer me a high five but I ignored it.

"Just shut up," I muttered, stripping my shirt off and rocketing it into my hamper. "We're idiots."

"Oh ease up, grumbly. We did one thing wrong. And besides, you shot a 31 and got an offer to Alcorn. Old man shoulda been proud as can be."

Maybe he was right. Maybe Dad should have been a little lighter on us. But he had always been like that and his system of fathering had worked pretty well, so far. Brian, Colton, and I were three of the best kids in town. Everybody knew it. We were well mannered because of our mother, well behaved because of our father, got good grades because we wanted nothing more than to get his approval and excelled on the sports field because he taught us to never back down from a challenge, no matter how big.

"That's exactly how he should've acted," I growled. "That's why we are who we are, today."

With that, I slipped out the door and turned on the shower.

CHAPTER 6

I woke the next morning, wondering if it was a dream.

The 31, the coach from Alcorn, the party, the car with Morgan, fleeing from the cops, our dad yelling at us, me yelling back. It couldn't have been real; not all of it, at least. There had to be some fragment of the night made up in my sleep, something that hadn't actually happened.

I closed my eyes and prayed I had dreamed the part where I yelled at my dad. I would have never done that, not in a million years.

My thoughts were interrupted by Brian, as he crashed into my room and fell onto my bed.

"Dude, I...am...so...freakin'...hung...over. It's killing me. My head's gonna' explode. I'm gonna' puke. Yes, I am gonna' puke."

He fell off the bed and crawled into the bathroom. As much of an idiot as he could be sometimes, he always found a way to make me laugh. There was never a dull moment with that kid. He began coughing violently and heaving. It was highly likely about half of it was real and the other half exaggeration but there was never any telling with him.

"You alright in there, hot shot?"

I burst out laughing but each laugh felt as if I were taking a 9-iron to the head and I tried my best to stop. My stomach lurched and I rolled out of bed and army crawled to the bathroom next to him.

"Dude, you gotta move, you gotta move," I pleaded. "Oh, God. Here it comes."

I missed the toilet completely. Maybe one percent of the vomit hit the rim of the bowl. It went everywhere. I looked over at Brian, who had rolled out of the way, and we both burst into laughter until tears started streaming down our faces. My head was pounding from it but it felt good to laugh.

I reached into the cabinet under the sink for some paper towels when I got a glimpse of my father, towering in the doorway, looking down at us, arms crossed, eyes glowering from under his half-moon reading glasses.

From our vantage point on the bathroom floor, he looked to be about nine feet tall. He didn't even say anything because, well, he really didn't have to. He just shook his head, made a grunt of disgust and slipped downstairs.

"That's what we like to call unfortunate timing," said Brian, still cracking up on the floor. "But seriously, dude, this shit is disgusting. You gotta clean it up. I can't handle it in here. I'm out."

He pinched his nose and raced out of the bathroom, leaving me with the splatter of vomit that smelled something like a combination of burnt hair and the wrestling locker room.

After close to an hour of hosing the floor with ridiculous amount of pine sol, windex, window cleaner, tile cleaner and bathroom cleaner and going through what seemed like 400 rolls of paper towels, the bathroom floor was reinstated to its former glory, aside from smelling like a damn car wash.

I showered, threw on a polo and khakis and plodded down the stairs. My hangover headache still throbbed against my skull.

Normally, a Saturday morning in the kitchen was a busy scene. My mother would be whirling around making omelets, Belgian waffles, pancakes, French toast, you name it, while my father sat at the kitchen table with a giant coffee mug, with a cheesy picture of Brian, Colt, and I when we were kids, in front of him. He would have a folded newspaper in hand, reading glasses on and, with a nod, would give us a curt, "morning boys" for a greeting.

However, the delicious scent of pancakes and old bay-laden eggs, which always seemed to make you hungry no matter how full your stomach was, were absent. The kitchen stood silent and vacant. The paper sat lonely, unopened on the kitchen table, still in its plastic wrap. Next to it was a note written in the sloppy, hurried handwriting of my mother.

"Sorry, no breakfast boys. Had a doctor's appointment. Your father took me. Wish me luck and I'll see you sometime later. Hit 'em straight. Love, Ma."

"Hey Bri. You see this?" I called to Brian, wandering into the family room and waving the note at him.

"Yea, weird," he said, not looking away from SportsCenter playing on our giant flat screen. "Didn't she say 'wish me luck?' What do we need to wish her luck for? Not to get lost?"

"Who knows. Glad we don't have to deal with Pops today, though. Couldn't have been better timing for a doctor's appointment."

He snorted and groaned, planting his face firmly into a pillow.

"When we playin'?" he asked, face still in the pillow.

"Let's just go right now, sweat this hangover out. I don't feel like waiting all day to beat your ass again."

Another snort and snicker.

"Sure, bro. Whatever, you say. You haven't had solid back to back rounds in your friggin' life. I'll put $100 on myself today."

He grabbed a hat off the back of the couch and pushed the brim down far enough so I couldn't even see his eyes.

"Either way, I don't see either of us playing any better than this hangover allows."

He slapped my chest on his way past me and stumbled out the front door. I just shook my head, grabbed a white Taylor-made hat to go with my electric blue shirt and white shorts and followed him, making sure to stuff as many water bottles in my pockets as I could before closing the door.

I thought my head exploded when I first stepped outside. The natural light from the sun sent my brain into panic mode. I immediately covered my eyes with my hand but then the reflection from the sidewalk caught me from the bottom and another wave of head pounding ensued and so went the rest of my round.

My swing felt like an unfolded lawn chair, as I scraped around the course, trying to survive the relentless beating of the sun. My sweat smelled like beer and by the time I finally collapsed back into my little Civic, after four miserable hours of hitting the ball nowhere close to the hole, my shirt reeked of stale, shitty keg beer.

"What a horrible choice that was," groaned Brian, as he slunk into the passenger seat next to me, smelling no better and looking even worse than I did. "Can't tell if I'd rather be dead or alive, right now. Either way, you owe me one hundred big ones. I got you by three, bucko."

I didn't even bother to respond. I just put the car into gear, pulled out, put the air on full blast, turned the music off. Essentially, I was going through Hangover Survival 101.

My dad's Tahoe was back in the driveway when we got home, as unwelcome a sight as any. The last thing I needed right now was a stern lecture from him about our irresponsible actions last night and our behavior this morning and how we're not living up to our family name and how we embarrassed him and yada, yada, yada. I sat in the car for a while with Brian, just closing my eyes and leaning my head back on the rest, mentally and physically preparing for the storm about to hit inside.

After about three minutes, Brian finally opened his door.

"Guess we can't hide forever, can we?"

So began the longest twenty-yard march of our lives up to our front door. Brian opened the door quietly, as if to sneak in unnoticed. Maybe it worked, I'm not sure, because we weren't greeted by a bellow from our father to get our butts in there or an annoyingly cheerful "hi boys" from my mother.

We slipped off our shoes before stepping onto the wooden kitchen floor, making sure to pick up any brownie points possible and tiptoed into the kitchen.

It was surprisingly empty. Lunch would usually be in the works at this point.

Brian turned and gave me a confused look. I shrugged and we began to make our way to the family room when Brian suddenly stopped. I nearly barged right into him before he turned around and grabbed me, his eyes wide and put a finger to his lips.

"Listen," he mouthed, gesturing to the right where I guessed my mom and dad sat in the next room.

"How are we going to tell the boys?" I heard my father whisper.

"I don't know. They are so grown up for how old they are. I'm sure they can handle it. But with Jay getting that offer from Alcorn and how well he's playing and then the party last night, they have a lot of things on their mind right now," my mother said in a hushed voice.

Brian turned and faced me and gave me a quizzical look as if to ask "What are they talking about?" but I just shrugged and pointed for him to listen again. Heck, if I knew.

"They're good kids I just..." there was something in my father's voice that I didn't like. I had never heard it before. Even though it was just a whisper, I could tell there was something off. It wasn't the commanding tone that demanded respect from any who heard it. It was vulnerable, weak.

My heart had that sinking feeling you get when you know you're about to hear some bad news. As when you get called into the principal's office or when your dad says "I need to have a few words with you."

"I just think we need to think of an easier way to tell them," my mother said.

My heart was in my throat now. What were they talking about?

Brian had enough of it. I tried to grab his shirt as he stepped into the family room.

"Tell us what, Pops?" he said, his voice a little shaken. As with me, he obviously could tell there was something not quite right here.

I walked in behind him and, judging from the looks of genuine surprise on our parents' faces, our quiet entry had worked.

"Tell us what?" Brian demanded again.

"Boys," began my mother, looking from Brian to me and back again. "Why don't you just sit down?"

Neither of us asked any questions. We slowly moved over to the couch opposite of them and took an uneasy seat.

"Your father and I, we…" she cut off, toying with her fingers as she tried to find the right words. "We…"

She gave a fleeting look at my dad, who put his arm around her, squeezed her shoulder and nodded. This was odd. They never showed affection. Maybe a kiss once or twice on their anniversary but they kept to themselves for the most part.

"We have some tough news for you and we're going to need you to listen and not be…"

Her voice caught and she sniffed. She blinked back what must have been tears. My mother never cried.

"Not be angry or upset or sad or whatever else; because, I need you to be strong. I need you to be strong for me, for your father and, most importantly, for yourselves and each other. Do you hear me?"

The pit in my stomach became a black hole. Something was seriously wrong here.

CHAPTER 7

In all considerations, I was an adult. Seventeen years old, a senior in high school, could drive a car, buy tobacco, pay my own insurance, was on the verge of becoming a college student independent of my parents but right then, I felt like a child.

I was a 5-year-old again. Tears welled up in my eyes, as the weight of her words set in.

"Breast cancer."

That's all my mother said. Her gaze wasn't soft or seeking pity or even remorseful, but strong and determined, like a boxer ready to begin a fight with a heavy favorite, set on making it last all 15 rounds.

It felt like there was a softball-sized chunk of ice in my heart. It took my breath away and I grasped for a grip on reality. I tried to be strong, to keep the emotions contained like my father had always taught me. I swallowed deep but my mouth was dry and scratchy. All the moisture was probably being welled up in my tear ducts.

"How bad?" Brian whispered next to me.

He was leaning against the wall, looking down at his hands as he always did when something stressful happened.

"Boys, it's not good. It's not good at all and, again, I'm going to need you to be strong and brave for me, for your father and for yourselves. You need to get a grip and you need to be there for me right now. I'm not going to spend my last days on this Earth watching you suffer. Do you hear me?"

"Last days?" blurted Brian. He had grown suddenly very pale. "What do you mean, 'last days?'"

My mother looked at my father. He nodded at her to continue.

"They caught it very late. It's my own fault. I should have gotten checked earlier and I didn't."

"How long?" I asked.

"Doc said about two months, maybe more."

She said it as calmly as if she was telling us when school would start.

Brian took a few steps back and held onto the wall. He had doubled over like somebody had punched him in the gut. I glanced over at my father, whose arm was wrapped tightly around her, now. His eyes were squeezed shut and his breathing came in uneven gasps. He was trying, and failing, to keep his emotions under control for his two boys.

Colton was hundreds of miles away on a football field, probably, completely shielded from the news. He would have handled it much better than Brian and me. He was always the one with ridiculous control over his emotions. The kid was tougher than anybody I knew, even of all my uncles in the military. He would have just nodded, wrapped my mother up in a hug, whispered some words of encouragement and promised to do everything he could to make her last days as comfortable as he could.

However, I wasn't Colton and neither was Brian.

Two months. That was it. She would never see me walk across the stage when I graduated from high school, would miss me picking up my diploma, would never hold her grandchildren and would never get to retire in a beach house in South Carolina as she and my father had talked about for as long as I could remember.

"So what does this mean?" I asked, looking up at her through my tear-stained eyes. "What's next? What do we do now?"

"Well, I can delay it, but it's too late to beat it. Doc says treatments can slow it by up to a month, but it's expensive and, with you heading to college soon, your father is going to need all the money he can get, especially without a second income. I'll do what I can but there's no point in wasting almost a year's worth of tuition for just a month of me suffering."

"Mom, I'll take loans, I'll work, I don't care. If you think I'm going to let you…"

"Stop, Jay," she said, cutting me off with a sharp look. "This is my decision and mine alone. I talked with your father and we decided this is what's best."

I sent a fleeting look at my father. He looked old and weary. The news was already taking a toll on him. There were heavy bluish rings under his eyes. The few wrinkles that were beginning to form on his face seemed more pronounced. His usually strong gaze was soft, weak.

"This is your mother's decision," he said tiredly. "It should go without saying that we, this family, will do everything possible to make her as comfortable as possible for as long as we have with her. We will pray and be thankful for each day we have with her. This is not a time to feel sorry for ourselves but, instead, be grateful for the amount of blessings we have received, thus far, in this life.

"Boys, I know this isn't easy. This is a lot to ask of high school kids who are busy running around getting drunk with their friends."

He paused, winked at us and grinned, just a tad. For the first time in what seemed like ages, although it had just been minutes since my mother had informed us she had breast cancer, I smiled.

How many kids could possibly have a family this loving, this devoted, this close?

"This is a time where you just need to be there for your mother."

I took a deep breath, used a sleeve to wipe off my face and gave my mom a long hug.

"Anything you need Ma, anything, you know we're here."

She squeezed me tightly and nodded.

"That's my boy. We're so proud of you."

I moved over and hugged my father. It was the first time I could ever recall doing so. I didn't say anything. Nothing more needed to be said.

I made my way past my parents and headed up to my room. I didn't close the door behind me, knowing Brian wouldn't be far behind and sat on the side of my bed. I stared into my blue carpet, thinking and waiting for my brother to come in.

Minutes later, he lumbered in and quietly shut the door behind him. I knew the news was going to be much tougher on him than it was on me. He was just a freshman, way younger than he ever acted. As much as he pretended to hate how my mother doted on him, cheered him on with unbridled enthusiasm, insisted on driving him to school and packing his lunch, his act would never fool me.

"Heavy," was all he could muster as he slumped down next to me.

"Yea," I responded.

I threw a long, lanky arm around his shoulder. His cheeks were lined with little creeks of tears, which dropped off his chin onto his shirt where a wet spot was already forming like an ink blot.

We sat on the side of my bed, him gazing absentmindedly into the carpet, letting his mind wander. I closed my eyes and let my favorite memories of our family together run through my head.

It was the little things she did that made her great—the waffles every Sunday morning for family breakfast after church, the overexcited claps after a routine par putt, the hours she would spend at the driving range with us when we were slumping, just watching and keeping us positive when we were most down, the standard "good luck, I know you will do great!" text messages before every match, test or miniscule presentation.

I smiled to myself, until a thought dawned on me that I had never really considered until now. She had done so much for us but what had we ever done for her? We said please and thank you, got good grades as she'd asked. But she had gone so far and beyond the duties of motherhood to ensure we were the happiest kids on the planet. And we had done…what, exactly?

My mind flipped a switch from reminiscent, complacent with making her last month or two simply comfortable, to the thought of doing something more, something…miraculous. I knew I wouldn't just walk into a chemistry lab and discover the cure for cancer but, maybe, we could help her forget about it.

I jumped up and off the bead and paced in front of Brian, clapping my hands together and bouncing like a sprinter in the blocks.

"What in the hell are you doing?" he grumbled.

I looked at him, still pacing, "What's the one thing Ma loves most?"

"I don't know, Disney World?" he shrugged. "She goes bananas for that place."

I laughed but shook my head, no.

"No, what's the one thing she loves the most? More than anything on the planet? More than Disney World, Christmas or the beach? The one thing?"

"Um, I don't know. She loves watching us play golf, I guess."

My eyes lit up. I nodded and motioned for him to continue.

"So what?" he asked.

He was clearly not following the path down which I was heading.

"What are we gonna do, bring her to the golf course every day to watch us play? I hardly think that's what she had in mind for her last few months, dude."

"No, not every day. Just two days, maybe four if one of us gets lucky as shit. Are you catching on now?"

His puzzled look answered my question for him.

"OK, she loves watching us pay golf but what's the one thing she said she wants to see her boys do? The one thing, dude. Just think."

It took a moment as he furrowed his eyebrows, thinking and staring into the carpet. And then the lightbulb went off.

"OK, I see what you're saying," he said slowly. "But how in the world are we going to pull it off? We can't just sign up, you know."

"Oh, I know a guy," I called back, as I raced out the door.

My fingers flew over my iPhone's keypad, dialing Mike Oberdorf.

CHAPTER 8

In his day, Mike Oberdorf was one of the best collegiate golfers to ever compete at that level. Victor at the U.S. Amateur, a record four times, he was considered a shoo-in as one of the all-time greats before he even picked up his first professional paycheck.

However, his heart was never really in it after he graduated from Alcorn, some thirty years ago as a four-time All-American. He accomplished, as he would tell people, "everything he could have ever imagined as a player." Tough to believe when that was coming out of the mouth of a guy who had never tasted Tour life or felt the sweet satisfaction of winning a major—or any tournament, for that matter. The millions he could have earned in prize money in just his rookie season alone was barely an afterthought to him. He said he had done enough with his golfing gift.

It was time to share that gift with others, to teach the game nobody will ever be able to master but one in which he came pretty damn close.

So, he turned down millions in endorsements from Titleist, Nike, Taylor-made, every company in the game and made Alcorn the happiest university on the planet by taking a head coaching position, practically for free.

As a player, he revolutionized the game. Young kids gave up football helmets for wedges, soccer cleats for putters because they wanted to be like Mike. However, this time it was a Mike not followed by Jordan.

As a coach, he nearly monopolized college golf. It was like UCLA under John Wooden. If you had even a sniff of a chance at playing at Alcorn, you went to Alcorn. You turned down full-ride offers from other prestigious and highly reputable schools just for a chance to walk on and sit the proverbial bench because you could tell people you'd played under Mike Oberdorf.

That was also thirty years ago. The zeal of playing for Oberdorf had certainly not been lost but it had dimmed. Alcorn was still the No. 1 program in collegiate golf, just not by the overwhelming margin it once had been. In his thirty years as an Alcorn coach, he witnessed twenty-two national title banners get hoisted in the rafters of the enormous basketball arena; he sent triple-digit players onto the pro tour, many of whom went on to become household names and he was named Coach of the Year enough times to the point nobody really seemed to care anymore.

Oberdorf was, and still is, a legend in the game of golf—bigger than the sport itself, almost.

For my current situation, it wasn't his mythical reputation or Yoda-esc teaching skills I was interested in—not at the moment, at least.

After I had bolted out of my room, leaving Brian bewildered behind me, I crashed down the stairs and found a spot in the basement, where my parents couldn't overhear me. I dialed Oberdorf's number.

It barely rang once.

"Jay," he answered, excitedly. "What can I do for ya'? You're not telling me you don't want to play for me, now, are ya'?"

Right, because who would ever want to play for Mike Oberdorf, I thought. I shook my head at his sarcastic yet earthy humor.

"Coach, I have a question, well, more of a request, and, um, it's a pretty big one," I stammered.

"OK, go on."

"Well, you see. OK, where to start…"

I paused.

For as quickly as I had formed the grandest of ideas in my head, I didn't even stop to think how I was going to ask him for this impossibly large favor. I had only known him a day, not even.

"Well," I finally mustered. "I guess I'll just tell you everything."

So, I did. For ten minutes, I told him about my mother being diagnosed with breast cancer, how she only had a few months to live and how Brian and I wanted to create this small miracle for her. He listened patiently and understandingly, adding a "mmhm," or an "OK" here and there to let me know he was still following. Finally, I got to the last part, the part where I would ask him to grant Brian and me each, a spot in the tournament he directed, the Coca-Cola Classic. It was the biggest of the non-major tournaments.

I stuttered through every word, hesitated worse than the kid in Billy Madison but I finally crashed through the request.

"You've got to be out of your damn mind."

In a cold and stony voice, that's how he responded. I never imagined such a tone could come from the jolly man, who had been inhaling chicken by the fistful just a few nights ago.

"Out of your mind. You two are a combined what, thirty-two years old or something? And you think you can compete with the pros? You shot a 31 one time, Jay, one time."

"I know," I whispered.

My once grand idea was suddenly crashing down on me like a house of cards. The tears made a flash flood back to my eyes. "I know, I just…"

"And you know what?" he continued.

His voice picked up a trace of the normal, joking, southerly one I knew.

"You're going to need a few more of those if you don't want to make me and both of you look like fools. After all, this is the Coca-Cola Classic and, not to toot my own horn here, but it's a pretty damn big deal."

"Wait," I said.

I paused.

"What…what are you saying?"

"I'm saying I love the idea, Jay. I love everything about it. Well, except for the fact that I'm taking two professional players' spots from an alrcady small field, which could potentially lose me millions in sponsorship money and earn me a few choice four letter words from quite a few people and maybe even get a few sanctions from the NCAA because this has to be illegal somehow but I'm not entirely sure how."

He chuckled a little at his own joke.

"But you know what we're going to do? We're going to worry about all that later, probably not at all really, because, well, I'm kind of well-known in this game and something tells me I have a little power over my own tournament. Now, let me talk to my tournament director and see what he says. Oh, wait, I forgot, that's me. Jay, welcome to the Coca-Cola Classic. And tell your cocky little brother he's in, too."

The phone slipped right out of my hands. I probably could have picked it up with my jaw. That's about how far it had dropped.

My stomach was doing more flips than an Olympic vaulting team, my hands shook with a bubbling, nervous excitement. I scrambled around the carpet to pick up the phone.

"Coach...coach are you serious?"

"Well sure. What better way to show the rest of the schools how terrible their chances are by sending you two out there—I'm counting on Brian, following in your footsteps to Alcorn by the way—to teach the pros a thing or two? Plus, your mother made a killer dinner the other night. I have to repay her somehow and I guess I only have a little while longer to do that so you tell her if she wasn't such a damn fine cook, she might have lost her chance."

I don't think my body knew how to react to the combination of the worst news I had ever heard to the best all in the matter of a few hours. I laughed. I cried. Tears zig-zagged down my cheeks and I couldn't tell if they were caused by laughter or sadness.

If there was anybody who could make a life-or-death situation somehow a bit humorous, it was Mike Oberdorf. Oh, but one nagging question still remained. It had nagged in the back of my mind since the idea began forming in my mind.

"What if we suck?"

The question was answered by a deep, contagious belly laugh that soon had me in a fit of that strange laugh-cry again.

"Trust me, that's not an option," he said between chuckles. "I'll see you tomorrow morning—five a.m., on the putting green."

With that, he hung up, leaving me stunned in a carousel of emotions. I didn't really know what to do with myself, so I just lay there on my cold basement carpet in a daze. I closed my eyes and soon my imagination began to whir, as any boy's would whose dreams were about to be realized.

"Now on the tee, Jay Lammey," boomed the dream announcer. The crowd went wild, roaring and chanting my name. My parents were inside the ropes, smiles wide enough to fit cantaloupes, pumping their fists and cheering me on. My mother looked strong as ever, tears of pride and joy streaming down her face. I blasted a perfect, arcing, left-to-right drive, which split the fairway.

The dream soon went into fast-forward. *I rolled in birdies, brought the gallery to its feet every hole, holed out from bunkers, walked in 45-foot putts. Newspaper headlines flashed:*

"Kid can do it all."

"Teen stuns field at Coca-classic"

"Oberdorf's boy charges atop leaderboard"

"Are you kidding me?"

It was the last one, though, that stuck with me from my fantasy tournament:

"The last 18"

I guess I had actually fallen asleep because, when I opened my eyes, they were crusty and dry. My back was stiff from the hard floor and my arms were thick with goose-bumps.

With a grunt, I sat up and scratched my eyes. I could feel the corners of my mouth begin to stretch into a sleepy grin. It stretched some more. This was actually happening. We were going to play professional golf. It had always been the one thing my mother wanted her sons to do, more than anything in the world.

I snapped up and raced up the stairs.

There was a lot to tell Brian.

CHAPTER 9

"You're an idiot," Brian grumbled.

He hadn't even glanced up from his apparent staring contest with my bedroom carpet. He just muttered those three words, with the emotion you might expect from a security guard.

I had been expecting this. This was typical Brian. He was always too down-to-earth to believe something like this could happen.

"What are you trying to pull?" he added, darkly.

This time, he did look up, breaking his fix on the blue shag to reveal red and puffy eyes. I had almost forgotten I should be feeling terrible, sad and depressed, maybe even a little angry, exactly how Brian was feeling, right now. A little bit of shame hit me when I realized how excited and happy I had allowed myself to feel just a few hours after learning that my mother was going to lose a battle with cancer, in a few months.

"You meet Oberdorf one time and now you think he's just going to magically place two kids in the field of one of the top tournaments of the year? A professional tournament? You're an idiot," he repeated.

"Hold on…" I tried to explain the situation to him but he'd brushed by me already, knocking my shoulder with his as he went.

Brian could wait. I should have known better than to drop the idea on him so fast. He was still young, after all. Just a freshman, although I always seemed to forget he wasn't my equal in age. He was far more mature than his friends, even if sometimes he did feel the need to act like a 10-year-old brat.

I let out a sigh and dialed up Colton. He always knew what to do with stuff like this.

"Hey, dude what's goin' on?" he answered cheerfully.

He was always happy to hear from me.

"A lot man, real lot. Brian's not taking it so well."

"Yeah, figured he wouldn't. Might want to give him some space. You know how he gets."

"Yeah. How you doin'?"

"Oh, you know me. I'm always alright," he said, but I could tell he sounded a little beat up. "After four years of suffering under that offensive line, Parkstead put in front of me there isn't much that can knock me down for too long."

We laughed and sat in silence for a few minutes. Memories of poor Colt disappearing under a mass of defensive linemen play after play after play flashed through my mind. He was probably recalling similar memories, only he was most likely wincing, not laughing.

"How did you do it?" I said, finally breaking the silence. "How in the world did you keep playing for that team?"

"Don't rub it in," he chortled. "You said there was a lot going on, what's up, Jay?"

"Well, I kind of made, well, thought of a present to give Ma. Kind of like one last big thing we can do for her, you know?"

"I'm listenin'."

"So, I'm not sure if you heard, but the other day I shot a 31 or whatever and the coach from Alcorn…"

"Mike Oberdorf?" he cut in excitedly.

Even for non-golfers like Colton, Mike Oberdorf was a name you just know.

"Nice, dude. Nice. So, what, he give you a scholarship or what?"

"Well, not exactly," I laughed. "But he did give me something way better."

So I told him about how Oberdorf granted Brian and me each a spot in the tournament, how that would be Mom's last chance to see us play, how I thought that might be the best thing for her—to spend her last days, watching her boys play professional golf. I felt a little bad, leaving Colton in the dark and, generally, out of the equation for our last gift to our mother.

"Well, I'm just going to be the shitty son who didn't appreciate his mother then, aren't I?" he chuckled.

"Yea, something like that," I joked. "I always told ya you should have picked up golf. You're gonna to have to soon anyways, old man. You've taken too many hits to play 'real sports'." I made my voice deep like his for that last part.

He always poked fun at us for playing golf instead of football.

"It's a sissy sport," he would mutter when we came home from practice fresh and full of energy, while he lay battered and bruised covered in ice, wraps and all sorts of bandages.

"But seriously, is this for real?" he said, switching back into serious mode. "This Oberdorf guy isn't just yanking your chain, is he? 'Cause I'll break his damn neck, if he is."

"Oh no, he's dead serious," I explained hurriedly. Colton had protective big brother syndrome.

"We're meetin' him tomorrow at five in the morning, for our first practice session."

"Oh, wowwww, he's getting you and Brian up at five in the morning?" he said, switching back into joking older brother mode. "That's a first, you lazy bum. Figures it takes a damn professional tournament to get you movin' in the morning."

I laughed and agreed. I'd never been a morning person. I had a feeling that was certainly about to change.

"Yeah…"

I trailed off.

"But I got to go find Bri and convince him this is for real, so he doesn't just not show up tomorrow. I can't imagine that would go well with Oberdorf."

"I have a feeling that might lose him that spot real quick," Colton agreed. "But awesome stuff, Jay, seriously. Proud of you, I gotta run, I'll talk to you soon."

"Thanks, Colt." With that, I hung up.

Colton was onboard; now I just needed Brian. He was always tricky. He could hit every extreme of the emotional spectrum in an hour.

I crept up the stairs and peeked around the right corner into the family room where my father was sprawled out on our couch, reading the paper under his reading glasses.

"You seen Bri?" I asked.

"Nope," he muttered, flipping the paper open and disappearing behind its pages.

I turned back and checked the dining room. Of course, he wasn't there. Nobody was ever in the dining room. I went up to the third floor, hesitating as I got to his door, the one with the chin-up bar nailed across the top. I gently nudged it open and tiptoed in.

He was sitting with his back against his bed, clutching something in his hand. His shoulders shook slightly, a mess of tissues lay scattered around his bare feet.

"Go away, Jay," he blubbered. "Just go away."

I stopped mid-stride. I didn't know what to do. He needed to know about the tournament. I knew Brian better than anyone did and I knew if he bought into what I had to tell him, what Oberdorf had blessed us with, he would be the Brian everybody loved, not the miserable, angry, snappy one that got him in trouble.

"Just hear me out."

"Jay. I...I don't want to do anything right now. I don't want to talk to anybody."

"Brian," I said, allowing my voice to rise slightly now. "We're all hurting here. Mom doesn't want you sitting in your room, crying, angry, shut off from the world."

Normally, calling him out like this would have resulted in an angry tirade. But crying has a way of sapping energy like nothing else. He was beat.

He turned around to face me. His eyes were so bloodshot you wouldn't even be able to describe their natural color.

He unclenched his hand and eyed what he had been gripping—a cross that had Joshua 1:9, our favorite passage, engraved on the top. In the bible, it reads: *Have I not commanded you? Be strong and courageous. Do not be afraid; do not be discouraged, for the Lord your God will be with you wherever you go.*

"I knew you weren't playing with me, earlier," he said, eyeing the cross as if he had just seen it for the first time. "I knew you actually got us in the tournament. I was just giving you a hard time."

He turned his eyes upwards to look at me and, finally, smiled his brilliant smile.

"The two kids who just got caught wasted underage, changing the world," he half laughed, half sobbed.

I grinned, squeezed his shoulder and made my way for the door.

"Oh, yeah," I called back. "We're meeting Oberdorf on the putting green at five in the morning."

"What?" he bellowed. I heard him spring to his feet and begin to hurtle after me, no doubt looking to beat me into a pulp for agreeing to such egregious practice hours.

I fled, amused and laughing once more.

Brian was in.

CHAPTER 10

The morning dew hung like a giant specter over the grass, so thick I couldn't see the rough five yards in front of me. In the thousands of times I'd played Everdeen Hills, I'd never seen the course like this—so serene, so peaceful, so…eerie. It reminded me of an empty church.

Then, the calm was shattered into a million pieces, like a motorboat roaring through a perfectly still lake.

"What in the hell are you boys doing?" bellowed a shadowy figure, standing where I guessed the putting green was. All I could see through the thick mist was Oberdorf's grayish outline. If I hadn't known any better, I'd have thought it was a ghost

"I told you to be here at 5 a.m. It's 5:02 and you're walking?"

Apparently, Oberdorf wasn't a morning person and apparently he was not a fan of tardiness.

"Sorry Mr…" I started but was quickly cut off by our clearly aggravated coach.

"Don't waste time with apologies. You've done enough wasting already."

I knew better than to try to explain and so did Brian, who was begrudgingly dragging along behind me. Oberdorf was similar to my father, frighteningly so. Off the field they could be your best friend. But on it, may the Lord help you if you talk back or make a mental error or, in Oberdorf's case especially, it seemed, show up late.

"I'd yell at you and give you some big pep talk about how horrible y'all look right now but that's just going to waste more time than you already have," he spat disgustedly, like his words were a poison he was happy to get rid of.

I still couldn't make him out clearly but I imagined he didn't have the rosy smile he'd had the other day. Even before we stepped foot on the green, he began barking out instructions.

"For the next two hours we're going to do nothing but putt. Every single one will be within twenty feet. Now, I will not make you late for school. I'm not that disrespectful to your teachers or your classmates, even though what you will be doing in two months is far superior to anything anybody in this excuse for a school system could possibly pretend to teach you.

"But you will complete this drill at some point today, whether it be before you step into your classrooms or before you hop in bed. It's up to you to do this and you only. I'm not a babysitter. I have other things I need to get to later and if you don't finish it on your own then this tournament is not for you and you should tell me right now, if you're in or not. Do you hear me?"

Standing a safe five yards away from him now, just far enough to get a whiff of the wondrous aroma of coffee, sneaking out from the enormous steaming cup in his hand, we nodded glumly. God, I wished I had thought to get coffee. I hated the stuff but it sure did work. I glanced over at Brian, who might not have heard a single word Oberdorf had said. His eyes were half closed and his head drooped to his chest. Apparently, he could have used it too.

Oberdorf studied us carefully through his watery blue eyes. I just awaited instruction and stared at the gloomy course behind him, still yawning awake with the morning. Brian continued his too-tired-to-care act.

"Well," he finally said, apparently not minding the half-asleep manner in which we had presented ourselves. "Do you want to know the drill you will never want to do ever again but are going to do every single day anyway because I say so?"

Once again, we nodded, too tired or scared to speak, in case we sparked another tirade.

"Wonderful. Now, Brian, you will be over here," he said, motioning towards a hole on the left side of the putting green. "And Jay, you here."

He pointed me to the back right portion, where my station would be.

"This is a race. From what I understand, you boys are as competitive as they come so I can only assume this will be finished within two hours. I once had a kid do it in half an hour. Would have never believed it if I hadn't seen it with my own eyes."

I still had no idea what we were doing. Judging from the look on Brian's face, he didn't have much of a clue, either.

"You will begin two feet away from the hole and go all the way back to twenty. Every time you make four putts in a row, you will move back two feet in distance. I have marked each distance with a tee from which you will putt next. Conveniently, this green worked out so perfectly that I was able to mix in flat putts, downhill putts, left breakers, right breakers, sliders and a few more, which would give any self-respecting pro cold sweats on a hot Texas day."

He paused, surveying us again, to see if we followed, before nodding. He continued pacing.

"If I see either of you so much as think about lining up your ball, one centimeter ahead of the tee, I will have you out of the tournament and off your own golf team before you know what hit you. If I see either of you so much as consider moving back after you fail to make four in a row, I will do the same."

Another glance at both of us.

"Have I made myself clear?"

We bobbed our heads in confirmation.

"Thought so."

He pulled out two blue, mesh pouches of balls for each of us to use for the drill.

"Well, good luck." He tossed each of us a bag and waved us to our respective holes.

"Twenty, says I get you," Brian called, as I pulled open my bag and let my four gleaming white balls dump onto the green.

"Don't you think you've done enough losing these past few days?" I taunted.

The 'dink' of a ball dropping to the bottom of the cup signaled he was done bartering. Twenty bucks it was then.

I studied my hole as I was figuring out a math problem. Oberdorf wasn't kidding when he said he had found pretty much every type of putt possible. My hole was on the top of a little slope, meaning he could have placed the tees down on the side of it for a very hard, very frustrating breaking putt, above the hole so it would be downhill and extremely delicate, below the hole so it would have less break but require a lot more force just to get it to the top and to the other side so it would be another tricky slider.

I found my first tee just a half step away from the hole on the left side—a little, breaking putt that would give me a nervous breakdown in a big tournament. I dragged each ball over one by one, with the back-end of my putter. I lined them up in order, next to the tee—about two inches in between each.

I made my first stroke.

'Dink.'

The ball had cut a path through the silvery dew into the hole, creating a perfect line for me to follow.

Another stroke.

'Dink."

And another and then another.

"That's four for four," I boasted.

"Congraaaaaatulations," Brian called back, sarcastically. "Two whole feet. Well done, well done."

He looked over and clapped loudly and obnoxiously, until Oberdorf growled at him to quit.

I went through my four and six footers just as easily, dropping each one dead center of the cup.

I glanced around to see if Oberdorf was impressed, but he wasn't even watching. He was on the other side of the massive green, toying with a wedge, his steaming cup of coffee on the shining, footprint-littered ground next to him.

I scooped the balls out of the cup and rolled them over to the eight-foot tee marker. As I lined up my Titleist, I heard Oberdorf cough loudly behind me. He was no more than two feet away. I stood over my ball. He hovered even closer. Then closer. He got to the point where I could smell the hot coffee on his breath, as if it were my own.

"You mind?" I laughed, raising my eyebrows at him and motioning for him to step back.

"Putt your ball, Jay," he said coldly.

He erased the scarce few inches we had left between us with another step forward.

I gave him a quizzical look and shook my head. The brim of my hat brushed his nose. I tried to return my concentration, or what was left of it, to the putt in front of me but all I could hear was his breathing so close to my ear. It sounded like I had headphones in, listening to static.

My thoughts were jumbled. I completely forgot what line I had chosen to take or how hard I needed to hit it.

I took it back and just as I was about to strike the ball, he clapped his hands right in front of my face. I yelped and nearly dropped the putter. The ball went skittering about three feet to the left of where I wanted and at least four feet short.

"What the hell was that?" I cried

"Good question. What the hell was that?" he said, an amused twinkle in his eyes. "That was the worst putt I've seen in a dog's age."

"No, what hell was that as in you clapping right in front of my freaking face when I was about to putt?"

Somewhere to my right, Brian was sniggering.

He clapped a meaty hand on my shoulder and gave me a stern look, much like one a father gives a son.

"This game is about mental toughness, Jay. If you let little stuff like that distract you as you just did, if you let that obliterate your concentration, you don't have a chance in the big leagues. Now, block me out, block Brian out. Block out everything except the eight feet of green lying between you and the hole. That's all this stupid, idiotic, awful game is: You, a strip of grass and a hole. That's it."

I pursed my lips and gave a curt nod and turned back to my ball. Oberdorf hovered again. He clapped and whooped, obnoxiously.

So much for that empty church feel.

I closed my eyes and took in a long, deep breath, drowning out the circus that Oberdorf was putting on next to me. Barely moving my head so as not to catch a glimpse of whatever it was he might be doing, I glanced towards the hole, back to my ball and made my normal, sweet stroke. The ball tumbled end over end on the exact line I had intended.

It disappeared into the cup with that honeyed 'dink.'

"Much better, Jay. Much, much better."

I was about to yell over at Brian again but Oberdorf cut me off.

"And, one more thing before I go drive your brother insane," he said with a wink. "when you win, say nothing. When you lose, say less."

With that he jogged—yes, an interesting sight to see a 300-plus pound man jogging on a putting green—over to Brian, taunting him with quotes from Happy Gilmore, as he went.

As I continued to line my balls up, putt, and repeat, I could hear the occasional whoop or holler or dog bark from Oberdorf over on the other side. I think I even heard a "cacaw cacaw." Often, these were followed by cries of anguish from Brian. I wondered how far he had gotten. I had just sunk my fourth ten footer, so I moved back to twelve feet.

I had lost all track of time. Oberdorf would pop in and out, sometimes watching me with his arms folded and nodding, sometimes throwing balls at me while I putted, sometimes banging clubs in front of my face, sometimes standing directly in front of the hole. Essentially, he was doing everything imaginable to keep me from making four in a row.

For all I knew, we had been doing the god-forsaken drill for nine hours, before Oberdorf called us over to where we had dropped our bags off.

"So, boys, don't you just love it?" he said, with one of those impish grins on his face.

Brian grunted. His arms were folded across his chest, his face in a permanent scowl.

"You'll thank me later Bri, don't worry. Just wait until you drop a little eight foot sliding putt to make the cut by one shot. You are certainly welcome for that. However, seeing as neither of you could finish the drill, you will have to return here after school instead of practicing with the team. I spoke with coach Hamilton and told him you were under my instruction for the day and he didn't seem to mind. So far, each of you has been putting for ninety minutes with Jay in the lead, sitting on his third 16-footer and Brian struggling to get passed his 12-footers."

A growl rumbled from where Brian stood. Oberdorf looked at him and smiled another wicked smile.

"Every day you do this drill, you will have the goal of lowering your time. So make sure to time yourselves and add this morning's ninety minutes to however long it takes you to finish out and let me know, so I can record it.

"For the record, you're both doing much better than several first-timers. Granted, I did bring pots and pans and even a few fireworks once…"

He paused and smiled, no doubt remembering the pain he caused some poor student.

"But still, you're doing extremely well, both of you. Don't get discouraged. If you are ever lacking in motivation to finish shitty drills like this one, always remember to think about the opportunity you have been presented. I mean, how many high-schoolers can say they played professional golf?"

He looked at us with his palms to the sky. A genuine smile was on his face, now.

"I know you're going to hate me for every second I help prepare you and that's all part of the job. But trust me, I know what I'm doing here and if you listen to me and do everything I say, you could do something incredibly special here."

There was just something about the man that made you like him. I mean, this guy just went from the top of my shit list to one of my favorite people in the world. I actually wanted to do his terrible, awful, dreadful, unpleasant drill just because I truly believed what he said.

"Well, we'll finish, eventually. I guess," I said.

He nodded and turned, calling back as he waddled to his car "Oh, I know you will."

School felt like it dragged on for about two days. I couldn't stop looking at the clock. My eyelids felt like they were made of concrete. Unfortunately, for me, I sat in the front of my biology class. We were studying Eucalyptus leaves and I had dozed off. More unfortunate for me, I twitched when I fell into one of these dozing sessions and, this time, I twitched so hard I sent my glass jar crashing to the floor. It must have shattered into a hundred pieces.

History wasn't much better. I tripped getting out of my desk and fell flat on my face. The only positive part of the day was lunch, where I opted to ignore my food in favor of a twenty-five minute nap outside on the school's patio. I wasn't sure how Brian was doing but, judging from how he looked this morning, he couldn't have been much better.

Even Mikey Cheyene, who was never big on doing people favors other than letting them wreck his house every weekend, asked if I was all right.

Morgan, who I still hadn't told anything about my mother or Oberdorf or the tournament, looked a little worried when we met at our usual spot at the senior lockers in between our third and fourth classes.

"You OK?" she asked, stroking my cheek. "You look exhausted."

"Yea, me and Bri have just had a long couple days," I said tiredly. "I'll tell you all about it later, just not right now."

She gave me a worried look and kissed me on the cheek before heading to class. I couldn't decide what I wanted to do less: go to class or finish Oberdorf's drill. I knew in the back of my mind I didn't have much of a choice.

I was convinced time had actually stopped during Algebra. Our teacher, Mr. Baker, an old, monotonous, bore-you-to-death skeleton of a man, droned on about functions and variables, I think. To be honest, I wasn't really sure. All my concentration was on simply staying awake, or relatively so, at least.

Somehow, eventually, the bell released me from my prison and off to the putting green again.

"Dude," muttered Brian, as he collapsed into my Civic. "This whole five a.m. shit ain't gonna fly. No way, Jose."

"Definitely not the best timing in the world."

Five minutes later, we were on the putting green again. Oberdorf's labyrinth of tees was somehow right where he had left them.

"At least, we don't have jackass clowning around this time," Brian muttered.

I silently agreed but decided not to talk bad about the man. He had, after all, granted us one hell of an opportunity.

The rest of our team came by to say hey before they played their practice round. They gave us confused looks at the dizzying array of tees in front of us. Our dark looks told them not to ask.

By the time my last twenty-footer disappeared into the cup, it was almost pitch dark. I closed my eyes, raised my arms to the star-speckled sky and breathed a "Thank you" to the heavens above. I looked over at Brian. He was still laboring over a sixteen-footer.

"How you doing, Bri?"

"Shut up."

I shrugged, walked over to my bag, dropped my putter in the bottom slot where it gave the most satisfying 'thump' and crumpled to the ground, waiting for Brian to finish.

The rest of the team had already come and gone. They had played their nine holes, put in an hour of short game work, wished us luck with whatever it was we were doing and headed out.

That was two hours ago.

A thought dawned on me as I lay on the cool, damp grass next to the putting green: homework. I debated grabbing my book bag from my Civic and studying while Brian was finishing out the putting torture but I was too tired. I would just wait until after I ate and had a little more energy.

So, I just gazed at the darkening sky and relaxed for about an hour while listening to Brian muttering curses and grunting every time he missed a putt. After maybe forty-five minutes of this, I heard him hammer-throw his putter with a "zinggggg." It was too dark to see where it landed.

He had finally made his last twenty-footer.

"We have to do that every day?" he asked in a rather pathetic voice. I had never heard him sound like that.

"I guess so. I mean, think about it if we do. We're never gonna miss a putt."

He agreed, with a reluctant nod.

"Wonder what Mom and Dad think we're up to. Probably gettin' hammered again, I would guess."

I couldn't help but chuckle. There was no doubt our father was assuming the worst, at this point, and our mother would be a worried mess. I felt a twinge of guilt at not texting her. She had enough on her plate, as it was.

Brian offered a hand and helped me up. I hadn't realized how much my back hurt from bending over my putter the entire day. It was caught up in a tremendously painful amount of knots. Nevertheless, Brian and I limped over to my little Civic, clutching our backs and groaning a bit with each step. Colton would have died laughing at the sight.

He groaned even more when he realized he had to go hunt for his putter.

I would have never guessed training for the 'gentleman's game' of golf would be so painful—and that was just the first day.

CHAPTER 11

Oberdorf was delighted to hear we both legitimately finished the first round of putting torture. He was even more amused to hear our father berated us for allegedly going to another party, which we actually didn't attend.

He didn't exactly buy our "we were putting for six hours after school" story.

"Well why would he believe you?" boomed Oberdorf in his contagious laugh. "You'd have to be out of your damn minds to practice putting for six hours. You two seem like you have your heads on straight so, really, you should be thankful he thought you were crazy. Would have been a bit odd if he thought it was just every day normal behavior. See what I mean?"

Over the next few weeks, Oberdorf leapt up the list of my favorite people. I'd never wanted to practice golf more in my entire life and it was hardly even because the tournament was coming up. It was because I wanted to impress him.

He pulled back the amount of times we had to do the first day's putting drill, which we had nicknamed "Putter-boarding" but sometimes I found myself wishing he hadn't.

I found that competitive drive had been passed down from my mother, actually, not my father, from whom most people would have expected it to come.

An All-American volleyball player in college, Janis Lammey had been an absolute stud, so much so that a cocky young man named Donald had chased her all the way from Kingdom Come to "Timbuk Two" and back again, just to get her name.

Most people didn't see that side of her often, just the fun-loving, overly enthusiastic, compulsive optimist. I knew better.

She wasn't surprised Brian and I had been going to the golf course before school, after school, devoting entire weekends to practice, skipping out on regular hangouts with friends.

One night, after we had completed the latest round of putter-boarding and were utterly exhausted, she pulled up in her clanky Explorer and took us out for ice cream.

After we were finished, our spoons scraping the bottoms of the paper bowls, the ice cream effectively demolished, she broke the silence.

"You know how I know you're my boys?" she said, with a bright smile.

I glanced up from my bowl and saw her deep brown eyes, still so full of life; I saw her thin arms, slightly emaciated but still lean and strong and I saw a face with happiness etched in every wrinkle and smile line.

"Because your father was all talent in college. He hated to practice. But you," she continued, wagging her spoon at Brian and me, "are just like I was. I could not get enough of the volleyball court. All day, all night, I was hitting, setting, jumping—doing whatever I could to be better.

"And I don't know what you boys have been up to at the course all this time but I know you're working hard and I just wanted to let you know how proud I am of you."

That my mother was dying was motivation enough for me to push through preposterously early alarms. The fire had already been there. She had just dumped gasoline all over it.

The next day, Oberdorf took us out to the 16th hole and dropped a ball about ten feet behind a twenty-five-foot tall oak tree. It still had a full collage of multi-colored leaves covering every inch of its branches.

"Hit it onto the green, inside that circle I painted around the hole," Oberdorf ordered.

The green was about fifteen yards behind the tree and a bunker guarded the front of it, so we wouldn't be able to get lucky by running it up under the tree and getting it onto the green that way.

For the first hour, we hit every single ball directly into the massive oak. It promptly spat them back at us, sent them careening off into a neighboring hole or scuttling into the bunker. Anyway, it wasn't going near the green, never mind inside the circle Oberdorf had painted.

The first time Brian cleared the tree we both celebrated as if we had just won the Masters. Then we realized he hadn't even gotten the ball on the green, or anywhere close to it. He just skied it about forty feet in the air and maybe twenty feet forward. Oberdorf scowled at us, arms crossed, eyebrows raised and motioned us to continue.

It took a few hours for us to finally land a ball inside the circle and we were both too angry to celebrate by that time just as we were too tired to even finish our schoolwork after the first night we finished Putter-boarding.

The next day, Oberdorf put us through a string of quirky drills on the driving range. He had us standing on one foot, hitting balls toward a sign one hundred yards away, until we'd gotten ten balls within a yard of it before we could switch feet and stand on the other leg.

When we finished that, he put a foam soccer ball under our inside arm and told us to hit balls that way for half an hour. We hit balls from our knees, we swung with our eyes closed, we swung without being able to watch where the ball went—keeping our eyes peeled to the grass below us so we didn't pick our head up too early.

But the one thing we didn't do once, was play golf.

"You'll get to that when I think you're ready," he would say when we pestered him about it.

"How are we supposed to know if we're getting better?" complained Brian. "Does he think he's the Mr. Miyagi of golf or something? Damn lunatic. And he's not even Asian."

Oberdorf would just laugh and mumble to himself, never giving us a straight answer.

It was in the middle of the third week of serving under the Oberdorf regime when we were allowed to play. Rather than give us his normal pep talk at the beginning of the day as he always had, he sent us a text in the morning that read: "Meet on the first tee immediately after school. Loser has to do Putter-boarding. Winner gets to go to the range."

I could hardly contain my excitement. I had forgotten how much I loved playing golf. Brian, still no morning person even after three weeks of waking up before dawn every single day, didn't have the energy to talk any trash quite yet, which was fine because I knew I would hear plenty from it later in the day. Sure enough, at noon I got a text from Brian as I labored through a history reading.

"Loser buys a thirty-rack of beer. No questions."

Loser also had to find a way to buy beer, seeing as we were both teenagers.

School crawled by as it had on the first day of our workouts with Oberdorf, only this time it was because I was too excited about the afternoon not dreading it.

Finally, the bell rung and released us to the course. We were the first car out of the parking lot.

"OK boys, I think you have earned this opportunity to get out on the course," Oberdorf said. There was that wicked glitter in his eyes, telling me this was not going to be the walk in the park Brian and I had thought it would be. "Now, just because you're playing today doesn't mean it will be a normal round. I will do everything I can to make you play the worst golf imaginable and I will do everything I can to turn your mental game to mush."

I wasn't quite sure what he meant but I found out soon enough. As I eyed up my tee shot on the first hole, Oberdorf sat cross-legged, no more than two feet to the left of where I had placed my ball.

"Am I bothering you here, Jay?" he asked innocently.

I knew better than to answer and fought to stifle a fit of laughs. He looked absolutely ridiculous: this enormous man, one of the all-time greats in the game of golf, sitting pretzel style two feet from a teed up ball, waiting for a high school kid to hit it.

"No, why would it bother me? You're so far away. Hardly even notice you."

But the thing was, I really didn't notice him. After all, the pot banging and screaming in our ears as we putted, all the things he threw at us on the range or revving up golf carts before our shots, this was a weak effort, so far as his distractions went.

I stepped up and ripped a titanic drive with that ball flight I so dearly missed watching. My little white Titleist winked at the trees on the left side of the hole and curved graciously back into the center of the fairway. It took a huge bounce forward and rolled another twenty yards to a point I had never been anywhere close to before.

"Oooohh, ahhh," crooned Oberdorf, with a low whistle. "Looks like somebody's been practicing."

I chuckled and put my big ole driver back in my bag and watched as Brian did the same thing, only his might have actually gone farther than mine. He picked up his tee, flashed me a cocky grin and looked back at Oberdorf.

"Good luck getting up, fatty."

I burst into uncontrollable laughter. Brian stumbled and nearly fell over as he grabbed his bag and ran from Oberdorf, who gave up his chase about fifteen feet into it.

"He's a bold one, your brother," he gasped, completely out of breath as I walked down the fairway, still unable to stop laughing.

That was generally how the rest of the round went. There was nothing Oberdorf could do to make us hit a bad shot. He threw a tree branch in front of me as I putted for birdie on the third hole but I still drained it. He did the YMCA next to Brian when he was chipping for eagle on the fourth and Brian still knocked it to inside a foot, despite shuddering with laughter.

He even organized a small army of golfers on the course to all yell obnoxiously at both of us as we made our approach shots on the ninth hole but we still hit the green as if it were any normal shot and actually had a pair of decent putts at birdie.

There was nothing that could stop us. For the first time in my entire life, I was completely in control of my game. There were no shots left up to chance, no possibility of making a terrible swing. I was one hundred percent on balance every shot because Oberdorf had us hitting those ridiculous one-legged shots for hours. When you practice hitting balls on one leg, it seems incredibly easy to swing with two feet on the ground.

His drills didn't seem so pointless anymore.

My swing was naturally condensed from when he had stuck the soccer ball under my armpit, which, unbeknownst to me at the time, had kept me from getting too loopy. Most of all, my putting was absolutely on point. If I had a putt inside twenty feet, I expected to make it. Even for the putts outside of twenty feet, I knew I had a legitimate chance to bury it. Prior to my meeting Oberdorf, I would just hope and pray for a two putt and a par.

By the time the round was finished, I had five birdies and four pars, another 31. The best part of it all—it was easy, this time.

I had only missed one fairway and that was by about two yards. I ended up making birdie anyway. I hit all nine greens, most of them ending up inside ten feet. I had thirteen total putts and every single hole I had a legitimate look at a birdie. Brian had done much the same, although his putting wasn't quite as spectacular as mine had been. Still, he finished with a 33 and, like my round, it had been so effortless.

In three weeks, Oberdorf had turned two decent high school golfers into legitimate players. There wasn't a single shot I stepped over that I thought I couldn't hit or a single putt I thought I couldn't make.

Oberdorf was waiting for us on the putting green when we put the flag back in on the ninth. He hadn't tried to distract us on the last hole and I guess there wasn't much of a point judging by how unsuccessful he had been on the first eight.

"Now, do you see what we have been doing all this time?" he asked, smiling widely. "Do you think I was doing all those things to make you look like fools for fun?"

Brian, even though he had lost to me and owed me a lot of beer and more than a few bucks at this point, just shook his head and laughed.

"Well, we did look like fools."

"No. You see all those hacks up there?" Oberdorf asked, pointing to the driving range where a couple guys, with some of the ugliest swings I had ever seen, were hitting balls. "They look like fools. What you just did out there today was beyond what I had ever hoped for and we still have another three weeks to get you ready.

"You made me proud out there today, I truly mean that. It was something else. Now, tomorrow, I'm going to give you the day off. However, there is one thing I want you to do and that's stay away from the golf course. Keep the clubs in the trunk. You spend tomorrow with your mother. I'm sure she hasn't been able to see you much and I want you to take her out to dinner or go shopping or see a movie or whatever. Just give yourselves a break from here and spend some time with her."

He looked at us through those beaming blue eyes and grabbed us each on the shoulder with a meaty hand.

"But after that, you're back with me."

The wicked grin returned.

"And we're going to work harder than we have because now I see just how good you boys can be. You can do something special at this tournament and that's a genuine statement right there. No hot air."

Brian groaned.

Oberdorf walked back to his SUV and sped off.

"I was so freakin' pumped about today until that," moaned Brian. "It was awesome playing like that, though. Felt like I couldn't miss."

"Seriously. I mean, what if we actually like, you know, win this thing?"

"Right, we're going to win. Sure, Jay, sure," he said, sarcasm dripping from every word. "Do you know how good those guys are? They don't miss shots. They don't miss putts. They would kick our ass every single day out here and you know it. We think we're hot shit by shooting a few under par today but they would be pissed if they shot that. We don't have a chance. We just have to do well enough to give Mom something to root for and then…"

There was something funny in his voice. It sounded like something had lodged into his throat. He tried to clear it.

"And then that's it, Jay. That's all she has."

I could see tears beginning to form at the corners of his eyes. He blinked furiously to keep them at bay but it was no good and a few escaped and ran down his cheek. He quickly turned his head, pretending I didn't see.

"And that's why we're going to come back every single morning and Putter-board or hit balls off one foot or army crawl eighteen holes or whatever it is Oberdorf thinks is going to get us better," I said, throwing an arm around him as we walked back to the car. "That's why we tried to hit balls over that damn tree for one hundred freakin' hours. You think I'd practice anything this much if I were just practicing for me? No chance in hell, dude, and you know it's the same case for you."

Brian finally looked back and nodded, his eyes bloodshot and puffy.

"This is much bigger than us. Think of all the people we can inspire. Think about the difference we can make not just in Mom's life, but in everyone's who hears our story."

Brian nodded and sat back in the passenger seat of the Civic.

"You should be an inspirational speaker or something," he laughed, tears still falling down his cheeks. "That was something. Do you talk like that to Morgan? I bet that gets her going, right there."

I punched him hard in the thigh, leaving a withering Charlie horse, which had him clutching his leg for the rest of the ride home.

CHAPTER 12

We were greeted at our door by the smell of pizza and wings. We found a six-pack on the kitchen table, with three empty Coors Light bottles next to it. A half-empty box of pizza lay open on the counter.

Brian just gave me a confused look and I shrugged. Neither of our parents drank much and we usually reserved pizza for weekends. I could hear the sounds of my parents laughing loudly over the television from the family room.

Hearing them laugh like that made me smile. I hadn't heard them sound so happy in a long time. My parents were tough nuts and had taken the news of my mother's cancer as if she'd just been told she was grounded for a few days but they had never acted like the happy, loving couple I knew them to be.

My dad, although usually reserved, had always given her a kiss hello and a kiss goodbye every morning he left for work. That had stopped since we found out about the cancer. They gave long, deep hugs now. They knew how short their time was together. Kisses were not enough.

My mom had stopped making us the incredibly huge breakfasts every morning. Brian and I were happy to settle for cold cereal before practice so she could get some extra rest but it was still so different being woken up by a screaming alarm clock rather than my mother's terrible singing and it was even stranger, eating in silence instead of going through our morning routine of a hundred questions.

What are you going to learn in school today? Do you have any tests? Did you do your homework last night? Did you double check the answers? What are you doing at golf practice? Playing or driving range today? When's your next match? Are you ready?

The questions went on for all twenty-five minutes between the time we woke, all the way until we escaped into my Civic and drove to school. Before, I had loathed them. I mean, they were the same damn questions every single morning. How could she possibly want to hear those answers over and over again? Now, I think I actually missed them. I hadn't realized how much the little things my mother did for us affected me but it had slowly begun to sink in and was finally hitting me like a ton of bricks now.

"Dude, you alright?" asked Brian, bringing me out my daze.

"Yea," I responded, half-heartedly.

"Is that my boys I hear?"

There was Mom.

Neither of us had to answer as our mother came crashing into the kitchen. Her cheeks were rosy and her eyes had a wild look in them I had never seen before. A glassy coating had started to form over them, almost like they were saran wrapped.

"Hi boys."

She wrapped us both up, half falling and half hugging us.

"How'd golf go? You guys have been spending an awful lot of time up there. Is everything OK with the team?"

Ah, all of her pent up questioning energy was now bursting out.

"Have you heard from Oberdorf? Coach Hamilton says he's out there working with both of you every day? Is that true? If it is, that's awesome. I'm so proud of you boys."

Judging from the look on Brian's face, he, too, was enjoying the swarm of questions she was firing at us. He had loathed her daily morning barrage. Now he was giving her a big hug, probably knowing there would only be so many more of her questions we would be able to answer.

"Ma," he laughed. "Hold on. You're drunk aren't you? I didn't know you were a drinker. Hey, Pops? You in there? You get Ma all hopped up on beer?"

A deep laugh rumbled from the family room and moments later, my dad stumbled in. His face was rosy too, although it was a little tougher to tell because his bushy brown mustache covered up a good portion of it.

"You know, Bri, I think we all earned a few beers these past few weeks. Go ahead," he said, motioning towards the remaining three beers in the six-pack.

Brian eyed him suspiciously, as if it were some sort of trick. He picked up a beer carefully, all the while keeping his eye pinned on our dad. Still looking at him, he slowly twisted the cap and took a baby sip. My dad just boomed another laugh and soon we were all drinking.

I could see why they were so drunk. When we walked into the family room, there were two empty six packs—the majority of the work was obviously done by my father—and a graveyard of bottles on the floor.

I'm sure the alcohol wasn't good for my mom's condition, but who cared? The thought made me recall a line from one of my favorite books, Tuesdays with Morrie. The old man in that book was dying, also from cancer, and he said, through death, he learned to live. Such seemed to be the case with my parents. My father was always cheery now. He was less bothered with us missing schoolwork and more focused on squeezing every drop of happiness he could in the final weeks with our mother.

Our mother was happy as always but she fretted less. The house was always a little sloppy, because she let us eat junk food and guzzle soda more often. She even let us cut class to go out to lunch one day.

The rest of the night may have been the happiest I had been in my entire life. We drank, ordered more pizza, played games, watched movies, prank called people. We called Colton and put him on speaker, talking about everything from his college football team to what he wanted for his birthday, in a few weeks.

As the night began to wind down around midnight—our parents had never let us stay up past ten on a school night—and the movie we had been halfheartedly watching finally ended, we were all exhausted and yawning. Even though I had been drunk my fair share of times before, I still felt that uncontrollable urge to spill mine and Brian's big secret. Alcohol has a funny way of doing that. We were planning to tell our mother tomorrow anyway but there was just something about being drunk that made me want to talk about everything I shouldn't talk about.

"Brian and I have something to tell you guys," I blurted out of nowhere.

My father drowsily turned his head, my mother snoring softly on his shoulder. Maybe it would be better if she found out later. I lowered my voice so as not to wake her, as if I were talking between pews in church.

"There's a reason we haven't been home much these past few weeks and it's not 'cause we've been getting in trouble or anything, which I know is what you probably think we've been doing."

Brian gave me a look as if to say 'What are you doing?' but I just shrugged and he nodded.

"We've really just been golfing. Mom was right, earlier, when she said she heard Oberdorf had been working with us. He has been—a lot, actually."

My dad was now sitting up, shaking off the drunken exhaustion and listening intently. My mother, well, she was sounding off a serious chorus of snores.

"We wake up at four thirty every morning and meet Oberdorf on the putting green and we practice until school starts. After school we go right back to the course and practice basically until we can't see the ball anymore."

"Is that why your grades have been dropping?" asked my father, leaning forward, a hint of anger slipping into his voice. "I know I've given you boys a little slack but if you think golf is more important than grades…"

"Dad, just hold on and let me explain. Just hear me out, one time," I said, cutting him off before he could explode into one of his angry tirades.

"There's a reason that Oberdorf's asked us to do this. And, really, he's been doing us a huge favor."

"Oh, c'mon Jay, just tell 'em already," said Brian, from where he was now laying on the family room floor.

I laughed nervously, still trying to find the right words.

"Alright, you know the Coca Cola Classic, right?"

"Sure, we used to take you boys there every year. Remember that one time you met Nick Eckard?"

"Yea, Dad, I remember," I laughed, thinking of how ironic it was that, in a few weeks, we would be playing against the very man we once hounded for autographs. "See, we're going back this year and you guys are, too. But this time…"

I paused, unintentionally letting the suspense build up.

"We're both playing in it."

CHAPTER 13

"Both of you?" my dad exclaimed.

His mustache twitched anxiously.

"So when you say you're playing in it, you mean what exactly?"

Brian was snickering on the floor below, while I struggled to get our father to realize what we were trying to tell him.

"Pops, he just told you," laughed Brian. "We're playing in it. You know, like hitting a little white ball around and trying to get it in some stupid hole, a few hundred yards away."

My dad scrunched his face together in concentration, as if trying to get to the bottom of some great mystery.

"Again, by playing, you mean what? Like you're in the field with all of those pros? Or you're just in the practice round or something because you're two good players? I'm still not quite understanding. You can't just say 'I'm going to play in a professional golf tournament' and they're just going to let you play."

Brian continued sniggering into the carpet and I was starting to chuckle too, which was not helping my father grasp what we were trying to sell to him.

"Dad, you know Oberdorf runs that tournament, right?"

He nodded.

"OK, well Oberdorf, for some reason, thinks Brian and I are the greatest kids on the planet."

He raised his eyebrows when I said that.

"Ridiculous," I said, putting my hands up in surrender. "Trust me, I know. But in all seriousness he thinks we can really be good golfers and, uh, I told him about Ma and her getting cancer and all and how she loves watching us play and…I don't know…maybe I sort of asked him for a spot in his tournament."

My dad just looked at me.

"So," he finally said. "You're telling me that in a week or two or however long until that tournament starts, I can just flip on the TV and Bam, there you boys will be, playing with the big dogs and Nick Eckard? That's what you're telling me?"

I just looked at him and shrugged. Brian, being Brian, said, "Well no, Pops. You're not going to flip on the TV because your freakin' sons are playing in a professional golf tournament. If you're watching on TV you got some issues, man."

He looked down at Brian then back to me then down to Brian and back at me, again, as if calculating where we were on his bullshit-o-meter.

"Where are the cameras?" he asked, patrolling the room, picking up random picture frames and pillows and studying them carefully. "Where are the cameras? Is this one of those horrible hoax shows you boys watch on MTV?"

Brian and I just stared in wonder, shaking with laughter as our father made his way around the family room examining lamps, books, pencil sharpeners, even the television.

"Dad," I finally said, as he was feeling around the edges of our flat-screen. "It's no hoax. You can call Oberdorf, if you want. It's for real. We're playing. I can tell you, we're pretty damn good now. I shot 31 today and Brian shot 33."

"You shot what?" he said, dropping the plastic cup he had picked up and was turning over.

"A 31 and a 33," Brian repeated.

Finally, he sat down, looking us up and down, again.

"How in the world? What's going on?"

Brian and I just looked at each other and busted out in raucous laughter, again. We had never seen our father like this. Maybe he was still drunk, I wasn't quite sure. I'd never seen him drunk so, maybe, this was how he was every time he drank. Sober, he was always so sure of himself. Now he was a confused old man, befuddled by his two teenage sons.

"Look, Dad, just go get some sleep. We'll tell you everything you need to know tomorrow."

"Tomorrow...aren't you going to be practicing all day tomorrow?" he responded smartly, as if finally getting his "gotcha" moment in our prank.

"We got the day off, so we could spend some time with Ma."

He looked confused again.

"Dad, really, tell you everything tomorrow. See you in the morning."

He just shook his head and scooped up my mom in his massive arms and trudged up the stairs. Brian chuckled softly from his makeshift bed on the floor and I collapsed back onto the couch.

I guess at some point we both drifted off to sleep, because when I woke the next morning the TV was still on, as were all the lights. My back was a little sore from sleeping on the quick-sand couch, inasmuch as it had nearly swallowed me whole by morning.

There were no sounds of my mother or father being awake yet and Brian was still snoring lightly on the floor.

It was peaceful, being by myself for once. For the past three weeks, Brian had been my shadow. Not by his choice, of course, but we had been together for every waking minute of every day since Oberdorf granted us the two spots.

So I soaked in my alone time while I could. I stepped outside on our back deck into the cool, fall morning. The air was fresh and a chilly breeze sent goose-bumps racing up and down my entire body. It didn't help I was still shirtless but it felt good, fresh.

I took a deep breath and looked into the sky, glowing a dim yellow as the sun began to peek up. I closed my eyes and did something I hadn't done in a long time, something that I probably should have been doing every day but had been too busy even to think about it. I gripped the cold wooden railings on my deck and bowed my head, taking in two long inhales to clear my mind. Then I prayed like I had never prayed before.

I prayed to thank God. I thanked him for blessing me with seventeen years of a life of family, friends, school, health and happiness. I had always taken these things for granted. Millions of people would never experience any of these things, let alone all of them. I was beginning to realize that.

When you begin to die, you learn to live.

I was not dying. However, somebody incredibly close to me was and those words had begun to ring true for me.

Next I prayed for my mother to live her last days free of pain. I knew this was unrealistic. I had seen the toll the cancer was taking on her—her appetite was gone, she was tired all the time, she often wasn't up to making her signature snacks. Nevertheless, I prayed, because that's what desperate people do sometimes—and I was desperate.

I then prayed for all sorts of things I hadn't prayed for in a long time—our troops, a friend who had been in a bad car accident, old Mr. Carl from down the street, Colton, Brian, my father.

I finished with the Lord's Prayer, took one last glance at the sunrise, blew a kiss to the sky and stepped back into the house.

That day, my father did something he swore never to do for as long as I had known him: he fibbed to get us out of school. He didn't know that my mother had allowed us to play hooky a week ago, but he didn't have to know. Let him feel generous. Not that he had much of a choice anyway, considering the news we had dropped on him last night. But still, it was something.

"Look at you, you rebel," Brian had shouted in the car, as our dad was calling in the "emergency doctor's appointment" for both of us.

That little comment nearly did Brian in. Our dad reached into the backseat with his free arm, all the while driving with his knees, grabbing Brian's left thigh so hard he was almost crying.

"I was just kidding," he mumbled, clutching his wounded leg, after he had been released from the vice grip.

We went to lunch, all four of us and put Colton on speaker phone while Brian and I explained the whole thing. Colt was quite amused by the conversation, having been already informed of our plan and was even more amused at our dad's reluctance to admit he had snuck us out of school.

Our mom, who had missed everything, snoring away while we told our dad about the tournament, was too shell-shocked to know how to react.

"Wait," she said, tinkering with her untouched salad. "Coach Oberdorf is getting you boys two spots in that tournament? That can't be right...we just took you there...it must be something different, right? I mean, that's professional. That's...that's a professional golf tournament."

When she finally finished her sentence and looked up from her salad to see the 1,000-watt smiles pasted onto our faces, she clapped her hands to her mouth and squealed.

"Ohhhh myyyyy goddddd,'

She flew out of her chair so fast she knocked it over.

"My boys are playing professional golf," she yelled to everyone within earshot, as she wrapped her now pencil-thin arms around us. "Oh my god, oh my god, oh my god. You're doing it for real? You did it. Oh my god, I'm so proud of both of you. So proud, so proud."

She wheeled to face my father, who was rumbling with laughter.

"And you?" she declared, pointing a bony finger at him. "Aren't you proud?"

"Well, I just pulled 'em out of school didn't I?"

She pursed her lips and nodded, confirming that was good enough for her and turned to extend her hug.

Normally, this type of display would have embarrassed the hell out of me. Today, I loved it. I beamed proudly to those around us who had turned their heads and were staring. Then I continued hugging my mom.

For the next few weeks, her energy returned to what it was before she had been diagnosed. Brian and I were, once again, greeted by the wondrous smells of waffles or pancakes or eggs in the morning and alarms were rendered useless as she made sure she woke us with plenty of time to get in a "big hearty breakfast before practice started."

I felt pangs of guilt, seeing her like this and that I had kept it from her for so long. She would have had something to look forward to this whole time but we had kept her in the dark.

Brian said it was for the best, that she would have tired herself out long before the tournament started and it might have lost a bit of its luster for her. I forced myself to agree. He was probably right. However, I couldn't help but recognize how much her extra energy seemed to carry over to our practices.

We no longer complained when Oberdorf told us to Putter-board or hit twenty putts in a row inside a three-foot circle from sixty feet away. We actually yearned to do it, for him to make it harder because we knew how much of a disadvantage we were at, being just high schoolers against the best in the world.

We wanted to make him proud.

There were even several practices for which we stayed long after Oberdorf dismissed us. He would just shake his head and laugh, call us golf's geek squad, and roll off in his silver SUV. We played a few more rounds in the days we outlasted Oberdorf, and every single one was even-par or better.

Even Brian was beginning to believe we could do some legitimate damage in the tournament.

"I mean, we never miss," he said, shrugging, as he effortlessly bumped a chip to within three inches of the hole.

I certainly couldn't argue with him. There wasn't a shot we couldn't hit and we knew it. The only thing we had to do was keep up that type of play until the tournament came around. My swing had a peculiar habit of disappearing around big tournaments.

Just one week before the tournament would tee off, Oberdorf called and said to meet at his house rather than the course. Brian, of course, registered a look of mock horror.

"Dude," he said after reading the text. "He might actually have a torture chamber over there. Just look at what he can do to us on the putting green."

We drove over, not really knowing what to expect. The sun hadn't risen yet, something we had grown accustomed to waking up to over the past few weeks and it was gloomy as we pulled up to his modest white house at the end of a cul-de-sac.

"This is his house?" snorted Brian, surprised. "He probably has more money than all his neighbors combined and then some."

I guess Brian expected a mansion. I knew better than to expect something overly grand from our coach. He was too down to earth to buy some towering home with lavish decorations, as so many big names in sports. He kind of reminded me of Chevy Chase's character in Caddie Shack, who would just leave $70,000 paychecks lying around his grungy old shack.

His lawn was about the size of a putting green and was mowed as such. It even had a little flag peeking up that said "Oberdorf" on it. The doormat at the top of the cement stairs was old and beaten up with faded green lettering reading "Sex is like golf: even when it's bad, it's still good."

Brian was about to make a joke about it when the door swung open and Oberdorf greeted us with his normal, booming "It's 5:01 and you're late,"

We just rolled our eyes and stepped in.

His walls were covered in pictures. When I say covered, I mean absolutely covered. I didn't even know what color the walls were painted.

There were pictures of him in college, of some of golf's greats, many people I didn't know— I'm assuming his family. There were signed memorabilia, a few medals and trophies were hung in cases, along with a handful of framed letters he had received and deemed important enough to give a spot on the overcrowded wall. One was from the president. I had just stopped to read it but he ushered me along,

"Nah, don't read that junk," he spat. "Don't know why I keep that stuff up there, anyway. It's just a bunch of words filled with hot air to make you feel good about yourself."

I looked at Brian, eyebrows raised. He just shrugged.

Oberdorf took us to his living room where a monstrosity of a television was mounted on the wall. He didn't say anything for a while, letting us watch football highlights and get a little comfortable before telling us what was up.

"Alright," he said, pacing in front of us, reflexively checking his watch. "Do you know why you're in my living room and not on the putting green?"

"Because we're so damn good?" asked Brian, innocently.

"Very funny, Brian. I'm amused. Now," he said, grabbing the remote and switching it to the Golf Channel, "We're here for this."

He moved to the side and turned up the volume to an old press conference that was being televised. I'm assuming Oberdorf taped it.

Nick Eckard was the one being interviewed, sitting at the podium answering questions with the same California-cool that Colton would.

"Oh, so we're practicing speaking?" said Brian, sarcastically. "That's a real doozie. And to think, I was terrified."

"This is no joke, Brian," Oberdorf snapped. "The media will rip you apart if you give them the chance and trust me, you will do just that unless you have a plan. Now, what's the plan here? How do you boys want the world to see you?"

I had never thought about this before. The entire world was going to know my name in a week. Well, for a few days anyway. I had always just imagined I would be myself. No plan, nothing to stick to.

"Do you want to be looked at as brothers who are two peas in a pod? Or, maybe you two want to be separate cases, not all that close. That's fine. Do you want the world to know about your mother and what you're playing for? I can make up any story I want for why I let you two boys in, I don't really care what the media thinks of me because they know what I think of them."

He smirked, probably remembering a witty one-liner he fed the press at a conference or something.

"Personally, I think you tell 'em right away about your mother. Now, I'm not one for pity parties and that's not what I want this to be."

He looked at us, waiting for a response, and, after not getting any, continued, "In my opinion, you tell them exactly the truth. Brian, I don't need you out there giving your tough guy routine. Just be the

fourteen-year-old adorable high school freshman—
the youngest to ever play in this event, mind you—
and everybody will love you. Jay, just do your thing
out there. You're smart, charming and selfless and
that's how the world should see you."

Brian tried to protest but Oberdorf silenced
him with a wagging finger.

"Now, neither of you have ever done this
before so you're going to need some practice or you
could leave this weekend looking like a bunch of
idiots, no matter how well you play, hear me?"

We nodded and he continued, "Alright then,
since you're not opposed, I brought a few friends
here to help us out."

"Alright, come on in," he called in the
direction of nobody in particular. Three men, all
yawning and clearly tired, dragged themselves into
the living room. I recognized the one sitting on the
far left. He was chubby, maybe in his mid-fifty's with
a balding head covered up by an orange Titleist hat.

His name was Tom Blubaugh, the local sports
reporter from the Parkstead Gazette. He was largely
regarded as a joke to most anyone who read him,
always getting facts wrong and half of the names he
tried to spell weren't even close to being correct.
Nevertheless, I liked him because he was always
friendly and kept his stories positive a hundred times
out of a hundred. I respected that because what's the
point in bashing a high school kid?

The other two I didn't know. They looked a
bit more professional. Both were dressed sharply in
button downs and ties, khaki pants and Sperrys.
Blubaugh just sported a plain white tee shirt and
cargo shorts complete with flip-flops.

"These men here are the type you will be seeing in two weeks," Oberdorf nodded, turning off the TV with Nick Eckard's smiling face. "This, as I'm sure you know, is Mr. Blubaugh from the Parkstead Gazette."

We nodded to confirm we recognized him and he gave us a tired smile in return.

"The next is Mr. Ferguson from the Associated Press, one of the few manageable blokes in their god-forsaken profession," said Oberdorf, clapping the man in the middle on the back. "And this last one here is Mr. Ryan from the New York Times.

"Now, Mr. Ryan is the one who obviously could do you boys the most damage, considering he has the highest circulation and is the most read sportswriter in America."

We shook hands with Mr. Ferguson and Mr. Ryan and sat back down.

"Mr. Ryan, being the most formidable writer here, will begin your training and Mr. Ferguson and Mr. Blubaugh will add instruction as needed."

Oberdorf stepped aside to give Mr. Ryan the floor. He looked surprisingly young for such an accomplished writer. He had a head of short-cropped, jet black hair and a pair of sharp brown eyes. He was tall and skinny; built like me except not quite as athletic and had a long, bent nose.

"OK," he said softly. "Now you men are new at this so I'm going to be easy on you."

His smile told me he genuinely meant that.

"Now, tell me what was going through your minds when you first heard from Oberdorf that you were being granted two spots in the tournament. For two high schoolers, or even pros for that matter, that's quite a big deal."

He looked at us expectantly and I glanced over at Brian, who shrugged. So, I began.

For the next hour we answered questions all about the tournament and our mother— about which Oberdorf had informed our three new journalist friends prior to our meeting—and golf, high school, homework and preparing for the tournament.

Blubaugh remained mostly silent, furiously scribbling notes and nodding along with our answers. Mr. Ferguson, a plump man, who couldn't resist repacking the bottom right corner of his lip with a new pinch of Skoal every twenty minutes, asked more difficult questions, making me squeamish.

"How would you feel if you shot a pair of 80's and missed the cut by ten strokes? Would you feel embarrassed or still happy for the opportunity? Would you apologize to your coach here?"

Oberdorf scoffed at these questions. He was protective of us and advised us not to answer. We gladly obeyed. I had no idea how I would feel in any of those situations. I could tell Brian loved being challenged. He had begun to answer several of them, and Mr. Ferguson sat up a little more attentive every time before Oberdorf silenced him and said "next question."

By seven, the journalists had left and it was just Oberdorf and us again. "Now, that was just a practice to get you ready but, mark my words, all three of them will have stories out on the pair of you before tonight and anybody who gives a damn about golf will know your names."

"So a practice interview counts?" asked Brian, suspiciously. "Why didn't you just say I brought three news people here to interview you instead of calling it training or practice or whatever?"

"Trust me, even with them writing stories, that's still just a warm-up. When the event starts with the practice round next Tuesday, you will be answering to hundreds of journalists. Luckily, you just took care of three quarters of any questions they could ask right here in my living room, without the spotlight of live television cameras and the pressure of answering in front of hundreds of people. This was the easiest way to get the bullshit out of the way."

Brian tried to say something but he knew Oberdorf was right. He was always right. It was things like this that made me appreciate Oberdorf. His plans were always mysterious and confusing and, sometimes, flat out bizarre, but they always had a point, much like his driving range drills and putting torture.

"Now, the tournament might not officially begin until next Thursday," Oberdorf said, "But the field comes out tomorrow and that means the rest of the world will want to talk to you. My advice? Don't answer. If you do, tell 'em you have homework or a test or something. They will eat that shit up.

"Let the stories that Mr. Ryan, Ferguson and Blubaugh are about to write, speak for you. They covered a wide range of readers from national, to worldwide to local, so you really shouldn't have to do too much more until you start playing. After that, you're theirs. My ultimate advice: let your playing talk for you. Even if you're terrible out there, which you won't be, trust me, keep your answers focused on the shots you hit on the golf course. If they try to detract from the tournament, by asking personal shit, always bring it back to the golf course."

All of a sudden, I was feeling overwhelmed. I was just a seventeen-year-old, a high schooler, who played high school golf, not professional golf. This was insane.

"Coach," I whispered sheepishly, looking at my feet. "But what if we do…suck?"

Oberdorf plopped down and wrapped his enormous right arm around me, which caused me to cave in slightly and looked me dead in the eye.

"You know why that's not going to happen?" he said, his piercing blue eyes more intense than I had ever seen them. "Because I've seen the work you boys have been putting in these past few weeks, and you know what? There ain't a soul on this freakin' planet who worked harder. And you know what else? You're playing with heart. And you're playing for something greater than fame and a paycheck."

I nodded numbly and he clapped me on the shoulder and stood up.

"Alright, well, next time I see you, you're going to be famous."

Brian and I both laughed at the thought; us, famous.

Oberdorf walked us out, warning us not to get big-headed and still meet him on the putting green after school.

"We still have work to do," he said, "Or all of this will go to waste."

CHAPTER 14

It felt like a couple thousand needles had just been jabbed into my face. I rubbed my right jaw, the side Morgan had just hit flush with a vicious slap and put my other hand up in surrender as she continued her onslaught.

"What the hell are you doing?" I shouted, in between blows.

An amused crowd had begun to form around us, as Morgan continued her incessant slapping.

"Hold on," I growled, grabbing her tiny wrists and pinning her against a nearby locker. In her left hand was a rolled up newspaper, which she had turned into a makeshift club.

"What is this?" she hissed, nodding to the paper in her hand.

I loosened my grip while keeping my guard up as she unrolled the paper, pointing to an enormous picture of Brian and me practicing at Everdeen. Under the photo, which took up nearly the entire upper-fold of the paper, read the headline "Lammey Boys To Play In Classic Next Week."

I yanked it from her hand and scanned the story, written by our chubby old friend, Mr. Blubaugh.

> "*Just two weeks ago, Jay and Brian Lammey were playing golf against high schoolers. Beginning on Tuesday of next week, they will find themselves up against the world's best at the Coca-Cola Classic, one of the most renowned tournaments on the professional tour and directed by Alcorn University head coach, Mike Oberdorf, who has offered the elder brother, Jay, a scholarship to play there.*"

"You didn't think I'd want to know?" asked a fuming Morgan, her hands on her hips. "How could you not let me know something like this, Jay?"

I glanced up at her, held up a finger to let her know I'd be back to her in a minute and returned to the story.

> "*How did two high school boys — Jay, a senior and the other, Brian, a freshman — get such an opportunity? The boys' mother and most devoted fan, Janis Lammey, had been diagnosed with breast cancer two months prior to the date the tournament was set to tee off. Her dream, according to her two youngest sons—they also have an older brother, Colton, who plays football at Watergate College—was to watch her boys play professionally. The doctors had discovered the cancer in its later stages and the Lammeys learned the news just a few months before it took its toll. Jay, a few days after receiving the offer from Oberdorf to play*

at Alcorn, called up his future coach and asked for a favor: two spots in the Classic so their mother could get to do what she should have been blessed to be able to do for years to come—watch her boys play professional golf.

Oberdorf, one of the most respected figures in the game, obliged and has had them on a ruthless training regimen ever since to prepare them for the daunting proposition of professional golf..."

Morgan yanked the paper out of my hand.

"How could you not tell me any of that?" she said, making a sad attempt at fighting back tears now. "About your mom, about the tournament, about everything…"

Her voice trailed off.

I didn't know where to start. I had made a conscious decision not to tell Morgan about my mother and without her knowing about that, I would have had to make up some elaborate and ludicrous story about how Brian and I got into the tournament in the first place. I hated telling lies.

"Look," I said, still unsure of where to begin. I glanced down at my beat up Sperrys, embarrassed, playing with my thumbs until she thwacked me with the paper again.

"Alright, Morgs. Here goes. I didn't want anybody knowing about my mom because people would have felt sorry for us and I didn't want that and my mom didn't want that and neither did Brian and my dad. That was how we wanted it. The fewer people who knew, the better."

I looked at her to see if she was following. She bit her lip and nodded.

"OK, now without you knowing about my mom, I would have then had to make up some crazy story about me and Brian getting into the tournament and you know that: one, I am a terrible liar and two, that's because I hate lying. I'm sorry I didn't tell you but I didn't tell anybody and neither did Brian."

I kissed her on the forehead and stooped down to look into her Easter egg blue eyes, which had opened the flood gates. Morgan was a crier.

"Oh, Jay I'm so sorry I shouldn't have hit you," she sobbed, throwing her lean arms around my neck.

"It's fine, really. Kind of woke me up. I needed that, actually," I laughed, rubbing my jaw in mock pain. "We've been up since like four thirty, so that was like a little cup of coffee…except it hurt a little more."

She laughed in between muffled cries and buried her head in my chest.

"So that's why we haven't hung out in…forever then?" she blubbered. "I thought you didn't like me anymore."

"No, no, no," I said, feeling twinges of guilt as I rubbed her back. I had been getting those guilty feelings a lot lately. "I should have said something to you, even if it wasn't the entire truth. I should have said something."

"Big meanie." She squeezed me tight and let me go as the bell sounded overhead, signaling we had two minutes to get to class.

"Can I take a look at this?" I asked, pointing to her paper. She nodded and handed it to me, gave me a kiss and took off down the hallway.

I read the rest of the story. This was the real deal. We were going to play professional golf. I had the proof right in my hands.

As the day went by, students, teachers, counselors and faculty members by the dozen stopped by to offer their congratulations. I had never seen or heard of half the people who came by to shake my hand but they seemed to know me pretty well, calling me by my first name, wishing me luck, the whole nine. I just went along with it. I smiled, said "thank you" to everybody, shook their hands. I was an overnight celebrity, probably the first ever out of Parkstead High.

Well, there was Brian, too.

"Dude," he muttered as he collapsed into the Civic after school had finally ended. "Holy shit. I mean good Lord, seriously. That was the craziest freakin' day of all freakin' time, I swear. I'm actually going to be thankful to get to the golf course where we can be at peace a little bit. I mean for Christ's sake."

I laughed, put the car in reverse and pulled out of the parking lot as kids pointed and waved at us.

We drove in silence for a few minutes, before Brian finally said it, a little too seriously for my comfort. "Jay, everything's going to change now, you know that, right? Everything."

I nodded. I had thought about this earlier.

"Mom only has so much time left and then what? We don't get sponsor's exemptions into tournaments anymore; we don't have the greatest Mother on the planet to take care of us. We have

Dad, and I love Dad, but it's just…I don't know how to say it…it's not the same."

I grabbed his shoulder and gave it a reassuring squeeze. Physical contact was the only way I knew how to comfort people these days. Words, it seemed, no longer fit the occasion.

"There's no sense in worrying about what's to come, Bri," I said softly. "All we can do is get as prepared as we possibly can for this tournament and take it from there. That's it."

We pulled into Everdeen's normally vacant parking lot, but today it was packed. Brian and I were looking forward to an escape from the madness. Our celebrity, it appeared, had followed us to the golf course. There was nowhere to park.

I glanced over to the putting green where Oberdorf would typically be staring at us and tapping his watch. Instead, there was a sea of people crowded around it.

"Oh, God," Brian grumbled. "I guess we have a fan club…and Jesus that's Jenna Doarn, dude. I haven't talked to her since we last…"

He couldn't suppress a grin and shook his head. "This is gonna' to be a nightmare."

As we trudged up to the putting green with our clubs strapped to our backs, more people we didn't know, would shake our hands, tell us what an honor it was to have us practice here.

"Good luck," they all said. "And make Parkstead proud."

We were the new pride of Parkstead. The only pride of Parkstead.

Brian and I were polite, we had been raised too well not to be, and we made sure to thank everybody for their wishes and we'd do our best. By the time we got to the putting green, the sea of students, parents, teachers were roaring with cheers and applause.

"Go get 'em."

"We're here for ya."

"That's my boys, Jay and Brian. Don't choke out there."

The last quip made me smile. I'd recognize that bear of a voice from anywhere. It was our Uncle Tito. He was a riot, that drunken uncle every family seems to have. He wasn't an obnoxious or violent drunk or anything like that, just a guy who wanted to have a good time—all the time.

"Uncle Tito," yelled Brian, dropping his bag and running over to hug him, slamming into his beer belly. Bri loved Uncle Tito. He was pretty much just a younger version of him, carefree and always looking for a good time. I was more disciplined and practiced, like my father but I still loved Uncle Tito to death. He and Bri were almost as close as Bri and I were.

"I'd shake your hand but it looks like they're full," I laughed, pointing to the two twenty-four ounce Coors Lights, in each of his enormous mitts.

"So bring it in for the real thing, brotha," he yelled. I could smell the beer on his breath.

"I made a little drinking game outta your little practice here," he rumbled, as I hugged him hello. "We'll see how rowdy I can get."

Of course, I thought. I laughed, punched him in the arm, causing a few precious droplets of golden liquid to spill out from his cans and I walked over to where Oberdorf was standing.

Per usual, he was smoldering at the opposite end of the putting green.

"Y'all done?" he snapped. "Or would you rather I'd set up a little Fan Appreciation Day instead of practice?"

He glared at Brian and then at me. We both looked down, our faces glowing bright red.

"Because in case you forgot, you two have four days until we head out. Four days to get ready. It's Friday right now, fellas. Friday. You have until Tuesday to become the best golfers you will ever become, you hear me? I don't need you dicking around with your friends and teachers and whoever else is here. I need you to be the two hardworking, focused men I've seen for the past two months or so."

We nodded and awaited his instruction. When he deemed that we were finally focused enough to begin, he ordered us to a round of Putter-boarding.

I made my way over to my side of the green where Oberdorf had already set up his labyrinth of tees. I dropped my four balls down beside the first tee.

I could feel knots beginning to form in my stomach as all my friends and a few teachers began gathering around to watch me putt. I smiled weakly and tried to look confident. I must have looked like an idiot, grinning stupidly at them and then missing the cup entirely.

"Get his autograph now. Go get it," yelled Oberdorf to my little fan section. "Can't even make a two footer but he's going to be great alright. Yup, go get it now, gonna be worth millions one day when he's a full-time cashier at Wal-Mart."

Nearly every single person in my little section was shocked that my coach could speak so caustically of me, which made me smile.

I knew Oberdorf loved us as sons. They didn't. Practice just wouldn't be the same without his constant verbal abuse.

I sunk the next four in a row and winked at my fans, who let out whoops of approval. Several were still glaring at Oberdorf, who had waltzed over to where Brian was putting. He didn't waste much time beginning his onslaught of Brian's mental game. Of course, Brian wasted no time in returning fire.

"I'll beat you any day, old man," he jeered as he moved over to his next distance. "Just like I'm about to kick ole Jay's ass, over there."

Well, if he did beat me, which he didn't, not many would have known. As the hours passed, fewer and fewer spectators remained until it was just us, Oberdorf, and our affable Uncle Tito, who had put together an impressive graveyard of aluminum cans.

That was our life for the next three days.

School remained a madhouse. Our cell phones became permanent ringers. Practice was a circus.

But then, Monday rolled around—one day left before the tournament's practice round was set to tee off. Our principal, Mr. Dolch, had happily obliged to our request to take off school for the week, asking for just a few autographed golf balls in return, an offer we were more than thankful to accept.

The Classic was at Olympiad Golf Club in California, way too far to drive, and Oberdorf had us flying on a private jet, loaned to him for the weekend by Alcorn. Our parents, Uncle Tito, and Morgan—I had worked her into the deal with Mr. Dolch, too—

were all making the trip. Colton couldn't take a week off of football, so would be remaining at Watergate.

Our small party, traveling to the Classic, met at Baltimore-Washington International Airport, BWI to anyone familiar with the area. We were greeted literally like celebrities. People in suits were there to take our bags, asking us if we needed anything. A security escort of men built like sharply dressed black vending machines took us around the runway to where Oberdorf was waiting for us.

I hardly recognized him. He wore a sharp, pinstripe suit, his hair was not hidden under his usual raggedy Titleist hat and he had dark sunglasses covering his eyes.

"Well would you look at this guy," whistled Brian. "I love the look, coach, love it."

Oberdorf rumbled with laughter and put two massive arms around us.

"Alright boys, I've done as much as I can do here," he yelled over the roaring engine. "This is all about you now. This is all on your shoulders. You've done the hard part, now it's time to sit back, relax and enjoy this terrible game we call golf."

He squeezed us in like a father hugging his sons and walked us into the jet.

This jet—or high class living room, or airplane, or whatever it was—was like something I had never seen before. This wasn't made for us. This stuff was for celebrities. This was for people like Nick Eckard, a celebrity, a professional, not two high school kids.

There were two columns of seats, like any normal airplane, but the seats were massive recliners.

I brushed my hand over them as I walked passed. They were made of suede.

Everything was covered in the navy and gold colors of Alcorn. The snarling Ram mascot was on the back of every headrest and there was an enormous blown up Ram embroidered on the carpet.

Towards the back of the jet, which could fit maybe twenty-five or so people, there was a poker table and a fridge stocked with sodas, water, Gatorade and beer. A waiter clad in white greeted us at the back of the plane and asked if we would care for anything to eat. We were too astounded by our surroundings to answer.

"I could get uuuuussseeeddd tooooooo thisssss," crooned Brian, running his hands over the incredibly soft seats. "This is absolutely unreal."

Uncle Tito grabbed a handful of beers and passed them around. My father glared at him from below his glasses but gave us the nod of approval.

"To the best nephews an uncle could ever ask for," Uncle Tito bellowed, holding up his Coors Light.

We clinked our cans.

I had hardly touched mine to the rest of the group before he was crumbling his up and cracking open a new one.

"This is awesome, Jay," said my mother, excitedly, as she sipped on her beer.

"It's incredible," I whispered, trying to soak it all in.

The plane roared to life and the pilot called over the loudspeaker for us to take our seats. I plopped down next to Morgan, who looked radiant in a dark blue dress, her blonde hair cascading down her shoulders. I kissed her on the cheek and she grabbed my hand, as the runway became a blur. She hated flying.

She didn't release my hand from her Kung-Fu grip until we were well into the air, the clouds looking like soft, cotton blankets beneath us.

"I love you, Jay," she finally said, looking at me with her impossibly blue eyes. "I just want you to know that, before you get famous and all."

She smiled and looked at me, hopefully. Morgan had never told me that before. I wasn't really too sure how to respond.

"You know I like you too, sweetheart," I said.

She couldn't hide the disappointment in her face. I knew what she wanted me to say but then again, I also didn't want to lie.

"I just haven't had much time to think about that kind of stuff, that's all," I added. "Once this is all over, and I'm allowed to hang out with you again without the big man over there taking up all my time."

"Heard that," growled Oberdorf, who was trying to sleep two seats back, his old hat back on his head and pulled low over his eyes.

"As I was saying," I laughed. "I'll have a little bit more time to spend with you, that's all."

Now Morgan was smiling that dazzling white smile, which had won me over since about third grade. I kissed her on the cheek and turned on my iPod. She went back to staring out the window as the marshmallow clouds passed beneath us.

I must have dozed off at some point because I was startled to hear the pilot's voice over the PA system again, announcing we would be landing in five minutes. My stomach began doing backflips and front flips and side flips and twists and turns and what have you. This was it. This was the real deal. When I stepped off the plane, I was going to be a professional golfer.

I shook Morgan awake and we looked out the window. Far below I could see the ocean and the beach—San Diego's I guessed—or heaven on Earth, as I would call it. I had always been a beach guy.

But I knew, somewhere down there, snaking in between the beach and inland, were super model-thin fairways, gnarly rough up to my knees, bunkers deep enough to bury a SUV, and enough water to drown my entire arsenal of golf balls. I took a deep breath and swallowed, smiled weakly at Morgan and put my iPod away.

In less than twenty-four hours, I was going to be playing the last golf tournament my mother would ever see me play.

CHAPTER 15

If I thought the jet was something, I had it all wrong. The jet was just the beginning.

Upon landing, we were picked up by a sleek black Escalade, with tinted windows so dark you couldn't see inside. We met our driver for the week, Mr. Mundie, a man the size of a Prius with a deep voice and tattoos stretching down both of his arms. I assumed he was either ex-military or a former offensive lineman but, quite honestly, I was too scared to ask him. He had greeted us with a grunt and a firm handshake. I responded by stammering out some sort of half hello half cough.

We cruised through the rolling suburbs of San Diego, occasionally snaking back towards the beach where we would get a glimpse of the never-ending ocean. I was too caught up in the sights—the sprawling mansions, views of the beach—to realize we had been driving for nearly half an hour when we reached our apparent destination.

In front of us was a palatial building complete with four white columns in the front. It looked like a giant fraternity house, except much nicer, as if there had never been a single beer cracked.

A couple of men were waiting for us where we parked. They grabbed our bags while a few scantily clad women in short, white dresses greeted us by first and last name and offered to escort us to our room. I smiled sheepishly. I looked over at Brian, who was grinning from ear to ear with a wicked glitter in his eye. He glanced back at me, winked, and eagerly followed like a puppy about to be taken on a walk.

I had no words. I just followed the beautiful brunettes, maybe a bit too eagerly because Morgan delivered a swift slap to my chin. Light but to the point.

It feels terrible to admit it but I had completely forgotten she was there.

"Jay," she said, staring up at the enormous white building in front of us and grabbing my hand. "Is this real? I can't tell."

"Yea," I laughed. "I think so. But I really don't know."

We walked up to the front and a pair of doormen dressed in all white opened the giant mahogany doors for us and we stepped in. It was an old school building, like a nice New York hotel that refuses to give in to the times. It had wooden floors and a crimson carpet. The salty but amazing scent of the ocean permeated my nostrils and I breathed deeply. I loved that smell. The brunettes took us up a spiral staircase and showed us to our room—or, mini-house, I'm not sure "room" quite fits the description. We had a kitchen bigger than the one we had at home, a mini-bar, an enormous flat screen that rested on the wall and four leather couches, each big enough to fit my 6 foot 4 inch frame. A balcony overlooking the ocean waited beyond the living room and on either side were a number of doors I presumed lead to bedrooms.

"Holy Shit," Brian exclaimed when the brunettes left. "Are you freakin' kidding me? Do you see this, Jay? Do you see this?

"Oh shut up, Brian," grumbled Oberdorf, as he trudged through the door. "All you're going to be doing in here is sleep so give it up already."

"Oh cheer up, Obi, there's a fully stocked fridge in there just for you."

Brian dodged a jab from one of Oberdorf's enormous hands, as my parents strolled in behind Oberdorf. They ogled just as I had.

We had never really stayed anywhere like this. We were just happy to afford a night at a Comfort Suites or a Holiday Inn. This was...out of our league.

"Alright," growled Oberdorf, as he returned back into the common room. "Everybody's bags put away and unpacked or whatever? Good. Let's go. We need to get to the course. Now."

He walked out and thudded down the stairs. I hadn't even had the chance to check out my bedroom yet. I scooped Morgan up off the couch where she had turned on one of her terrible reality television shows and I carried her into what I assumed to be our room. That's where the brunettes dropped our stuff. I nearly dropped Morgan as soon as I saw our view.

To the left of our bed, which was the size of a small pool, were sliding glass doors that led to our own private balcony and a telegenic view of the San Diego beach and the blue ocean beyond. I couldn't help myself.

I stepped out onto the balcony and leaned against the railings, breathing in that sweet, cool ocean air for just a moment. Then Oberdorf was back. He grabbed me by my collar and dragged me out of the room.

"Did you come to vacation or did you come to play golf?" he growled.

"Golf, sir. Golf," I mumbled.

Morgan broke out into a fit of giggles as her 6 foot 4 inch boyfriend was towed roughly out of the room by a 300-pound man.

"Have funnnn," she called, as Oberdorf slammed the door shut and nearly threw me down the stairs.

"Easy, easy," I sighed. "I'm going."

The three of us were back in the Escalade again with grumpy ole Mr. Mundie. I guessed our clubs were in the trunk. I hadn't seen them since we'd pulled into the airport back in Baltimore.

"OK," Oberdorf said, finally sounding a little more pleasant. "Sorry for the gruffness back there but it had to be done. I've seen far too many players get caught up in all the materialistic bullshit and fancy schmancy crap and then play terribly and not even care because they had been so pampered they lost sight of why they were playing in the tournament.

"Now, you boys remember what you're here for, right? Or rather, who you're here for?"

This was the first time Oberdorf had ever really mentioned our mother. He had always made it about us; probably, because he'd never dealt with a situation as delicate as ours but whatever the reason was, he'd usually kept it about us and the golf course, nothing else.

Brian and I both nodded. I could tell he was feeling as guilty as I was because of how quickly we had been caught up in all the "fancy schmancy" stuff. For a brief moment, we had both completely forgotten that we were here for our mother.

"OK. Mike Keane, you boys know him?" he asked. His question was answered by our blank stares.

"He's the director of course management at Olympiad and he's taking over most of my duties as director, inasmuch as I'll be spending most of my time with you boys. He's also the one who will set up the course and let me tell you, it's not gonna be pretty. This isn't going to be a walk in the park."

Of course, neither of us expected it would be a walk in the park. This wasn't Everdeen Hills and this wasn't Parkstead. This was professional golf.

"Now," continued Oberdorf, "this isn't going to be a tournament won by the spectacular. It's going to be won by the lack of unspectacular—you know, spraying balls into the water, duffing chips, missing two-foot putts, the sort of shit that's so easy for young players whose nerves go to mush. You need to manage out there, grind. Don't try the miracle shots. Accept bogey, give yourself chances at par. Keep the numbers small. If you avoid a terrible shot, you avoid the big hole. You avoid the big hole, you avoid the bad round. You avoid the bad round, you make the cut. Don't play like an adrenaline-hyped kid who thinks he can perform miracles because he's playing for something more than everybody out there combined. This is your chance to do something special."

This, I supposed, was why Oberdorf was always so successful. He may not be the most likeable guy at times but he sure as hell knew what he was talking about. I sure as hell intended to listen.

The Cadillac stopped and Mr. Mundie opened the doors. Four boys about me and Brian's age grabbed our bags and hustled them over to a stand next to about 20 others. Our bags looked rather puny in comparison to those belonging to the pros. Each one was the size of a mini vending machine with their names neatly monogrammed on their bags along with the names of their sponsors.

Me and Brian's name tags were both faded and red, with "Parkstead Golf" monogrammed on them. They were small enough for most anyone to carry with just one hand for eighteen holes.

"Well that's embarrassing," snorted Brian. '

I just shrugged and laughed.

"Welcome to the big leagues, I guess."

Oberdorf led us around the castle, which was the clubhouse, past the 100-yard putting green where a dozen or so pros were practicing, past the driving range where a good portion of the field was working with their personal swing coaches and past another smaller green for chipping and bunker work and, finally, into the back entrance of the clubhouse.

We were greeted again by a group of stunning brunettes.

"You boys must be the Lammeys," said a golden-tan and incredibly pretty one.

I tried to say "yes ma'am" but it came out something like "yes'm." She giggled and checked us off a list, handed us passes I guessed would be our lifeline to everything this week, and wished us luck.

"I'll be rooting for you," she said with a wink, which melted my heart into a puddle of wax.

"She liiiiikkkkkessss you," crooned Brian.

I tried to laugh but it came out as a splutter.

"Shit," Oberdorf mumbled as we picked up our bags and awaited his instruction. "We didn't think about getting you boys caddies, did we?"

The thought had never really crossed my mind. I had never had a caddy before. Why would I now?

"We'll be fine," I shrugged. "My bag's as light as a peanut and I'm seventeen years old. I think I'll live."

"No," he grumbled. "On this course, you need a caddy. Hold on."

He disappeared back into the clubhouse and chatted animatedly with the stunning brunette. I couldn't help but use it as an excuse to gawk at her some more.

Brian shrugged and walked over to the chipping green. I reluctantly followed. We lazed through a few drills for a couple minutes before Oberdorf reappeared with two kids who looked about twenty or so. Oberdorf hurried them over to where we had stationed ourselves.

"Jay, meet Tim. He's going to be your caddy for the week. Tim meet Jay," he said, introducing me to the taller of the two.

"Nice to meet you, dude," I said, shaking his extended hand.

Tim stood about three inches shorter than me but considerably more buff. His forearms were thick like a baseball player's and his broad shoulders reminded me of a kid from Reagan High. He had short blonde hair as I did and his blue eyes matched mine. He was dressed in all white with the golden "Olympiad" mountain logo on the right side of his polo.

Brian's caddy, James, was hairy and sweaty. He spoke slowly and coolly and used the word "bro" four times in his first two sentences. Perfect for Brian.

"OK, now that you're acquainted," Oberdorf said. "Let's get things started."

So we did. We went through an hour of chipping, chatting casually with our new best friends for the week. Tim was a junior at the University of Southern California, studying journalism. He played basketball for USC, hence his muscular and athletic frame. But, from the way he acted, you'd never have known he was a D-1 athlete. He was soft-spoken and humble, never answering when I asked him about his best games or most points he ever scored. Right off the bat I knew I liked Tim. I also didn't really want Morgan to meet him. He was too much like me, only with a lot more muscle.

James and Brian got along equally well. They high-fived and laughed, "bro" this and "bro" that, with every shot. James was also a student at USC but didn't play basketball, although he jokingly claimed he was an intramural all-star.

After we chipped, Oberdorf took us to the range where we worked on shots one hundred-yards and in for an hour, before delving into the longer stuff. Tim was shocked at how far we could hit the ball. Oberdorf was more concerned at how far we could hit the ball in the wrong direction.

"You can get away with that at Everdeen," he would say. "This isn't Everdeen."

Several reporters had lined up behind us as we practiced, scribbling notes every now and then. We hit balls until our arms were tired and our swings started getting a little sloppy. Oberdorf noticed and said it was time to take 'The Tour'. A few reporters tried to ask us questions as we were leaving the range but one look from Oberdorf shut them up.

It was beginning to get dark but Oberdorf insisted we see every possible angle of every possible shot. I had only seen the course on TV, so it was truly something to see close up.

The first hole was a straightforward par-4, long but nothing menacing. Bunkers guarded the front of the green and the fairway was bordered by rough, which had been grown to mid-shin height. This, as I would later find out, was the easiest hole I would see.

The second was a devil of a par-5. It doglegged left off the tee and cut sharply back to the right, making going for it in two a reckless endeavor meant only for a Sunday charge.

The third was a two hundred-yard par-3, with the ocean racing up the entire right side of the hole.

Actually, the rest of the front nine was lined by the coast. I had seen plenty of balls do cliff-dives into the Pacific. Even at 7 p.m., a considerable wind was blowing. I couldn't imagine what it would be like during the actual tournament.

Tim and James pointed out nifty tricks and what spots to avoid and where to make sure to miss if we happened to do so. Missing in the right spots was the key to managing a round. Even if it was rare, missing in the wrong spot could come with a three-stroke toll. Missing in the right spot was maybe a one shot drop. That was what makes or breaks a player in a tournament. Tim and James made sure we knew that.

After two hours of walking, it was pitch dark and we could no longer see anything more than a few yards in front of us. Oberdorf finally relented, taking us back to Mr. Mundie and our slick Escalade. He instructed our two new friends to meet us on the putting green at seven the next morning and they nodded and left as we hopped into the car.

Morgan was sprawled out on the couch, watching the Kardashians when we got back. She said our parents were taking a stroll on the beach. When they returned about an hour later, my dad was holding a bottle of champagne and my mother was smiling like I had never seen before.

My dad called for a toast.

"To a family I could never have dreamed of having," he said, with misty eyes while holding up his glass. "No matter what you shoot out there, this is the proudest I've ever been in my entire life."

We clinked glasses and sipped our bubbly. Our father motioned for Brian and me to join him on the balcony. We followed him. The three of us just stared into the cool, dark night for several minutes before he finally broke the silence.

"I don't know what to say to you. In two months, I have seen you grow from boys to men and this has made me..."

He began to choke up.

"It's made me…"

He couldn't finish. I hugged him tight.

"I know, Dad, I know. And in two days we're going to show you just how much we've grown—out there on the golf course—because we're going to win this thing."

CHAPTER 16

The next day was largely the same, although this time our practice round/walk-through teed off in the morning when we could truly marvel at Olympiad's beauty.

The palm trees, lining every hole, looked like they all had been taken from post-cards. Every hole seemed a perfect spot for a wedding, I thought.

There wasn't a single blade of grass out of place. Trust me, I looked. The rough was thick and gnarly; the bunkers deep and unforgiving, filled with blinding white sand.

What truly stood out to me, which hadn't really the night before, was the incredible undulation of the greens. A long putt could break three different ways. Even the shortest of putts wouldn't be a gimme.

Every hole featured a plateau, a hill, a drop-off or some sort of ridiculous sidewinding break. There were so many spots on the green where the pin could be placed that Brian and I took close to twenty minutes examining and reexamining each one. We went back and forth like we were navigating grocery store aisles, keeping our heads down the whole way, surveying every possible bump and break.

The course was truly an astonishing achievement for whoever designed it. It was gorgeous and deadly, picturesque and precarious. It made me think of a Siren's song.

What I really loved about Olympiad was, unlike many courses, there were no holes that would punish a good shot. Your score would reflect how well you played. Bad shots were damning but you would be rewarded for good ones. Some courses, such as Everdeen, had slants on the fairways, which would send even a perfectly placed ball careening into a stream or the woods.

We grabbed some lunch from the never-ending buffet after our walk-through, which preceded our normal routine of putting and chipping and range work. By the time seven rolled around, we were too tired to do anything positive to improve our swings.

All we could do was wait.

The whole family, including Morgan and Oberdorf—at that point, they were both considered family—went out to dinner that night. We went out to a restaurant, which Oberdorf recommended and it lived up to his unbridled praise. We feasted on steaks, ribs, shrimp and salmon before the waitresses brought tubs of ice cream buried under mounds of chocolate cake.

If Oberdorf's plan was to have us eat ourselves to sleep, it worked. Normally, even before high school matches, I wouldn't get a wink of shuteye. Tonight, however, hitting the sack was all I could think about. My stomach felt like it had a basketball pressing against it. My eyelids were heavy and drooping.

Unfortunately, Brian and I had drawn a later tee time, 11 a.m. We had never heard of our playing partner before, some guy named Stanley Conner. I had googled his name as soon as we found out about the pairing. He seemed like a good fit—young and talented but still relatively unknown in golfing circles.

"You need a drink to fall asleep, champ?" called my Uncle Tito, as I headed to bed. "I know how you get nervous."

Brian had already accepted his offer and was midway through his second beer.

He wasn't himself.

He was quiet and jumpy, laughing nervously at jokes that weren't funny and didn't return fire when somebody poked fun at him. He guzzled his beer and reached for another.

"Atta boy," exclaimed Uncle Tito, thumping him on the back so hard nearly a quarter of the beer flew out of the bottle.

I grabbed a can from the fridge and sat down next to Brian.

"You alright?"

"Dude," he said. "What if we suck? On national television. I mean, it doesn't really matter if we choke in high school because it's high school. But what if we freakin' suck tomorrow?"

I hated when Brian got like this. Every now and then he'd become the greatest pessimist anybody had ever seen. It usually happened when he got nervous, which, if there was any time he had a right to be nervous, it was now.

"So what if we're not any good?" I said, with a laugh. I was surprised at my own confidence. "So what? Who cares? So we suck the next two days, who's going to say anything to us? What will they say? 'Oh, you guys suck because you lost to the best players in the world?' No. Nobody's gonna say that. We have absolutely no pressure at all. Sure, it would be nice to play out of our minds for Mom but that's not what we're here for. We're here just so she can see us play. That's it. She won't care if we suck and neither should you or me. We're way overmatched and everybody knows it. That's why I'm goin' to go to bed and sleep better than ever 'cause, for the first time I can remember, neither of us can be expected to win. If we get dead last, we're still better than every other high school player in the world. We've already won."

The familiar grin I knew so well was forming back on Brian's face now.

"I told you, you shoulda' been a motivational speaker or something."

We cheered, chugged our beers and said goodnight to Uncle Tito, who had plopped down onto the couch and was flipping through the movie channels.

My dad and Oberdorf were on the main balcony, drinking and talking about the tournament.

My mother, constantly tired now, had called it an early night.

"What are the odds they make the cut?" I heard my dad ask in a hushed voice. I waited for Oberdorf to answer.

"Honestly, Don, not high. But not low either."

I had never known what Oberdorf actually thought our chances were.

"Most kids I push that hard, just fold and quit. Your boys didn't do that. They stuck with it through all my bullshit and carrying on and insane drills. They are the best golfers they could possibly be at the point they are in their careers. I truly believe that."

Brian had heard this, too. He was smiling easily again.

We stepped outside, clearly catching them off guard.

"You should be in bed," Oberdorf growled.

"Just saying goodnight, you grump," Brian said.

We hugged our dad tightly and high-fived Oberdorf before heading back inside.

"Don't forget to bring you're A-game," Brian called, as he headed to his room. "I can't have my older brother tarnishing the Lammey name out there."

I shook my head, shut the door and crawled under the covers next to Morgan. I hoped the real Brian would show up tomorrow morning, too.

I didn't sleep nearly as well as I thought I would. I must have awoken fifty times, each time sprinting to my phone to check the time, convinced I'd slept in.

Judging from Brian's bloodshot eyes the next morning, he had done the same.

"Are you boys ready?" exclaimed my mother, from the kitchen. I could smell eggs, bacon and sausage.

She abandoned her post in the kitchen and gave me a big hug. She was so frail now. Her arms were scary-thin when she hugged me.

"Just remember how proud of you we are," she said, running over to Brian to give him a hug as well. "This is so exciting."

She hurried excitedly back to the kitchen, half bouncing, half running, and Brian and I plopped down on the couch and pretended to watch TV. SportsCenter droned on in the background but I didn't hear a word. It was nothing more than white noise.

I was busy imagining a million possibilities: I was winning, draining every putt, crushing every drive, paring every iron; then I was losing and losing bad, hitting balls out of bounds, whiffing, shanking shots. I shuddered at the thought.

My mom brought over two heaping plates filled with eggs and bacon and sausage and handed one to each of us. She patted some old bay seasoning—Maryland's pride and joy, and we never left the house without a canister of the stuff—on top of the eggs and told us to dig in.

"Here they are, America's soon to be most famous teens," roared Oberdorf, as he strode out of his room.

"Riiiiight," said Brian through a mouthful of food.

"What's this, more Lammey cooking?" he asked pleasantly, rubbing his belly. A minute later, he sat down next to us with a plate piled higher than Brian's and mine, combined.

"You boys ready?" he asked, digging into his enormous mountain of food.

We both just shrugged.

"Ready as we're gonna be, I guess," I said.

"Atta, boy."

Nevertheless, as we cruised to the course, my nerves began to lose control. I wasn't ready. How could I be?

Mr. Mundie didn't help either, when he kindly said he would root for us not to shoot more than 100. He laughed at his own joke.

When we got to the course, it was an entirely different scene than the one we'd been welcomed to the previous couple days. The cart boys were still there to take our clubs and put them on the rack and there were the familiar faces of Tim and James, which eased my nerves a bit. However, there were now hundreds of media vans and reporters. Fans flocked by the thousand not to the course itself but just to the driving range.

The grandstands behind the greens and tees, largely vacant and bare during the practice rounds, were now swarming with people wearing bright polos, people wearing dark button downs, women wearing skirts, women wearing jeans, young kids, bigger kids, old men, middle-aged men, kids my age, kids Brian's age. It was madness.

Even crazier, in my opinion, we had a police escort to get us through the crowd. The one encounter I'd ever had with the police wasn't exactly pleasant but these guys were friendly enough and even wished us luck as they dropped us off at the putting green.

Even there, hundreds of people gathered around, craning their necks to watch the 20 or so other players that were practicing alongside us.

I tried to steady my breathing but it was becoming increasingly difficult. My inhales came in hoarse gasps and my exhales were wheezes.

"You OK, brothaman?" Tim asked.

"Yea, just uh…this is insane."

"I feel you. First time I got in a game at USC I tried to take my warmup pants off mid-stride, you know, to be cool or whatever, but I tripped and fell flat on my face. Crowd loved it. Teammates haven't let me forget it since. Just be thankful you don't have to take off any clothes in front of these people."

I laughed. That was one thing I didn't have to worry about.

The more putts I hit the more my nerves began to settle. Oberdorf had left us for the time being to go glad-hand some important-looking men dressed in suits. I guessed they helped run the tournament or something.

He met us at the range a half hour later and helped us work out some stubborn, last-minute kinks in our swing. We hit balls for maybe thirty minutes, until a man in the Olympiad all-white uniform approached us. He had a round, friendly face and jet black hair that peeked out from under his Titleist hat.

"You boys ready?" he asked, pointing to the watch on his right wrist. "You're on the first tee in ten minutes. Best to start making your way over there now."

I looked at Brian. We laughed. We smiled.

This was actually happening.

"OK, professional golf, here we come," he said.

The man smiled and leaned in so nobody else could hear except for us and our caddies.

"For what it's worth, I'm rooting for you," he said, tapping the left side of his black hat, which bore the pink breast cancer ribbon. "I think what you're doing is incredible. Go get 'em."

We thanked him and he turned and led us to the tee. As we walked, I began to notice an overwhelming amount of breast cancer ribbons. They were everywhere: people's socks, hats, shirts, pants pockets. I even think I saw some temporary tattoos. Maybe they were real, I had no way of knowing.

Several fans called us by name, telling us they'd be rooting for us. More than a few eagerly reached over the ropes, presenting towels and other various objects for us to sign. Oberdorf ushered us quickly along and I mouthed "I'm sorry" to as many as I could. I wondered to myself what my autograph would be worth after this tournament.

Probably nothing, right?

The man in all white led us behind the grandstands and beside the first tee, where there was a table full of candy bars, energy bars, Gatorades, waters and sodas. He politely asked us if we wanted anything but Brian and I quickly said no. I knew for a fact that I wouldn't be able to stomach anything.

Tim handed me my driver. I pretended to examine it as the seconds ticked by, painstakingly slow. I recognized Stanley Conner, our playing partner, when he got to the table, introduced himself and his caddy and shook our hands.

We made small talk about nothing, discussing the trip from the east coast and whatnot, and then I heard it.

"Please welcome to the tee: from Parkstead, Maryland," boomed the elderly starter. "Mr. Jay Lammey."

The crowd roared in approval as I stepped up and placed my ball on the tee. I hadn't yet looked at the grandstands behind me.

In hindsight, it was a terrible decision.

It was packed. People were waving towels, flags, posters, hats. They howled and clapped enthusiastically, whistling and cheering. I didn't know what else to do so I raised my hand to acknowledge them and they grew impossibly louder. I looked for my parents and Morgan and Uncle Tito but couldn't spot them among the thousands of faces. They were here somewhere.

I turned my focus to the hole at hand. It was easy, I knew that much. During the two walk-throughs, I had seen every possible angle and shot I could ever have. I knew, as long as I kept the ball down the right side where the rough was not as deep and the palms didn't cut me off from the green, par would be routine. But, no matter how much I assured and reassured myself this was an easy hole, my stomach turned into an Olympic gymnast, flipping a thousand times per microsecond.

I shook my left arm out and stepped up to my ball. The crowd died down. The only noise was the footsteps of people walking between holes. One more, a deep breath.

Then I swung.

Surprisingly, I made flush contact with the ball. I watched as it sailed down the left side of the fairway, leaving me nervous for a few seconds—it wasn't coming back, but then it did.

It was oh, so perfect.

It sunk back to the right and, after rolling for about twenty yards, stopped dead center of the fairway. The crowd was deafening.

"Nice," said Stanley, clapping me on the back as the starter called his name and he teed up his ball. His drive missed down the right side of the rough but it wasn't in any real trouble.

Then Brian's name was called. I had never seen him so pale. Normally, he coveted this type of attention. But now, he was shaking and rattled. Sometimes it took scenes, such as this, for me to remember he was just fourteen years old.

He glanced over to me. I gave him a nod and mouthed "c'mon."

He nodded back and stepped up. However, his nerves took over his swing and did their worst. He flared his ball way out into the left rough, right in the middle of a group of towering palms. He was shut out, almost an automatic bogey.

Nevertheless, the crowd rained down "whoos" and "go get ems" and "we're pulling for you's." They loved us and I already loved them.

"Here we go, I guess," grumbled Brian, as we trudged down the fairway together.

"It's just one shot on one hole, dude. Who cares?" I answered.

"Yea, bro, just one shot," piped in James. "No problem. We'll get you outta those stupid trees and put it in the fairway and get up and down."

By the time I got to my ball in the fairway, Brian had disappeared into the crowd and the trees. Stanley had found his ball resting just into the rough.

"Better start than my basketball career, brothaman," Tim laughed, as we stood in my absolutely perfect position in the fairway.

"Yea, but you only played a couple minutes in your first game," I said, still fighting the butterflies racing around in my stomach. "I'm about to play four hours."

"More time to impress 'em, then."

I took a step back to see what I had in front of me. The pin was on the front-left side of the green. Not the toughest spot by any means—but I was hardly thinking about making birdie. I stood maybe 150 yards away, just an easy 9-iron. I didn't want to go long and have an impossible chip coming back.

Stanley's ball ended up on the back right third of the green and I wasn't sure what Brian was doing over in the woods. I asked Tim to hand me my 9-iron. I stepped up to the ball. Silence greeted me once more.

I wasn't nearly as anxious to hit the ball as I had been on the tee and I stood over it for a second, taking a deep breath before putting a smooth swing on it. Again, it was flush.

Too flush.

The ball sailed clean over the flag and somewhere either on the green or over it. The latter would mean almost certain bogey, the former a tough par.

"Let's hope that stayed on," I grumbled, as I handed the club to Tim, who wiped it down and slid it back into the bag.

"Oh, it did, trust me. I'd say you'll have a thirty-footer. You have more room back there than you think."

He was right on the money. I didn't pace it off for the exact count but thirty feet couldn't have been too far off. Brian had punched his out into the fairway and chipped up to about seven feet for his par. Stanley had at least a seventy-foot putt for his birdie, a stroke less than par for the hole.

While he prepared for his putt, I stalked mine. It was downhill, very downhill. It would be NASCAR fast and likely have to hit the hole to stop anywhere within five feet of it.

"It's delicate," murmured Tim, as he crouched behind my ball. "You're gonna have to hit this like you're hitting a five-footer, brothaman. Best to lag it, not try to make it."

What if I did make it? What if I started out my professional golfing career with a birdie? How loud would these fans get? How insane would that be?

"Don't even think about it," Tim said, picking my brain. "It's not worth it. Get your par and get outta here."

I reluctantly agreed. Stanley had hit a brilliant putt to a few inches and he tapped in for his par. The crowd clapped, politely.

Oberdorf's drills had always taught me to make putts but this wasn't a drill and missing had real implications. No reset button.

So, I hit it softly, knowing full well it wouldn't be firm enough to hold its line all the way to the hole. The crowd groaned as it slid two inches too low but no further than tap-in distance away. I exhaled.

The crowd's groans were replaced by another chorus of ear-splitting roars and whistles when I tapped in for par. I smiled and waved back, letting out another exhale. The nerves were gone.

Brian, however, could not say the same. He had put a yippy stroke on his putt and cursed loudly as it missed badly below the hole. He nearly blew his two-foot comebacker, too, but it curled in at the last second and the fans let out collectively relieved sighs and clapped loudly for him.

"Don't worry about it. One hole, dude. Thirty-five more," I said.

He muttered incomprehensible things to himself as he rushed by with his head down and hands stuffed into his pockets. My nerves had been tempered and it showed. To the delight of our faithful following, I parred the next seven holes. Brian, however, was still trying to find his swing.

He had hacked his way to two more bogeys and a double and hadn't hit a fairway yet. Not even James could cheer him up as his mood went from dark to black to completely toxic.

He was falling apart.

Then, on the ninth hole, we found them. My parents, Morgan, and a beer holding Uncle Tito were standing just outside of the ropes on the ninth tee. All of them were clad in pink tee-shirts and Titleist hats with the breast cancer ribbon logos on the front.

"You're doing so great," my mother squealed over the crowd.

"Hey, Bri, cheer up would ya? It's just golf," boomed Uncle Tito.

Finally, Brian relented with a smile. This is exactly what he needed. He dropped his driver and hugged our mother—the fans stood up in appreciation—and gave a fist-bump to my Uncle Tito.

"Now," Brian said, that cocky glint back in his eye and the wicked grin back on his face. "Let's play some golf."

Just like that, he became the Brian Lammey with whom I'd grown up playing. He didn't hesitate to steal my honors on the tee, piping a drive down the middle without taking so much as a practice swing.

Stanley didn't appreciate Brian's rediscovered self as much as I did. When Brian got cocky, his etiquette suffered considerably. He routinely teed off before he was supposed to and often hit his shots when he wasn't technically the farthest from the hole.

"Your brother's kind of a dick," Stanley grumbled on the 13th hole.

I just laughed.

"Yea, but you gotta love him."

Stanley's mood had worsened as his play declined. He had yet to birdie a hole and had suffered four bogeys before doubling the 12th, considerably slimming his chances of making the cut.

Brian's round went quite the opposite direction of Stanley's. He made the first birdie of anybody in the group, walking in a twenty-footer on the 13th.

He sent the crowd into a frenzy.

With the confidence he had after that, bogeys were out of the question. He rallied like a veteran, paring his last five holes to finish with a 75. By pro standards, it was a pretty piss-poor round but for us, it just meant he wasn't out of it yet and that's all that mattered.

I had allowed just one bogey the whole round to go along with 17 pars. It was pretty boring as far as scores go, especially with the numbers I had been putting up recently but I still finished three shots ahead of Brian.

We tapped on the 18th and shook hands with Stanley.

I looked immediately for my mother. She wasn't tough to spot. Wrapped in my dad's arms, she was bawling her eyes out. Somebody had given her a tissue box and she was rifling through tissues by the second.

"I'm...so...proud...of...you," she sobbed.

At that moment, I had completely forgotten what I had shot. This is what we came for. Brian had the biggest smile on his face I'd ever seen as he ran over to hug our mom. I followed suit and the six of us—me, Brian, my dad, Morgan, Uncle Tito and my mother—were one big lump of a hug on the 18th green.

The crowd went ballistic. Some whistled, some cheered some even cried.

"Wonderful," Oberdorf exclaimed, running over, jiggling the whole way and clapping Brian and me on our backs. "I'm incredibly proud. A one-over and a four-over? Are you freakin' kidding me? That's fantastic."

He glanced over at my mother, whose smile was impossibly big and her cheeks were stop sign red from laughing and crying so hard.

"And look at her," he said, pointing to my mom. "Look at that smile. Look at that. Couldn't be any happier with you boys, either of you. You've earned it."

"But coach," I said. "We still have another day to make the cut."

"Yes, you do," he said, still beaming. "But you've already accomplished what you came for. Look at your mother's face right now. Just look at it."

I did and he was right. This was everything we had come for. This was why we woke up before dawn and came home after dark every day for the last two months.

Above all else, the one thing our mom had wanted to do her entire life—watch us play professional golf.

I took a step back and surveyed the scene in front of me, my Uncle Tito hugging my dad—the two never got along, Brian laughing with Morgan, Oberdorf congratulating my mother. I smiled big.

We did it.

Now there was one more thing we had to do.

Win.

CHAPTER 17

"Dude," Colton yelled from the other line. "Tell me you're watching SportsCenter."

Colton hadn't been able to join us on the trip. He couldn't just take a week off football.

He was following us, of course, but at this point, it was hard not to follow. We were everywhere.

Oberdorf had instructed us to agree to every post-round interview and be pleasant, charming and humble. We talked to a few reporters, even our old dip-spitting friend, Mr. Ferguson and had a press conference but I didn't think we would make any news.

My 72 placed me in the mid-30's and Brian's 75 was buried so far down the leaderboard we didn't even bother checking. I wasn't quite sure why we made the news but they gotta fill the papers, right?

"You guys look stupid on TV," Colton chuckled. "Everybody here is going nuts about it. You're famous—imagine that, my baby brothers, famous. Who'd a thunk it?"

Morgan had flipped the television to SportsCenter and there we were, front and center, answering questions in our press conference after the round.

"Do I really look like that, Colt?"

I never knew how skinny I was. My arms looked like string beans.

"Nah," he said, pausing, "Much worse."

I laughed and it made me realize how much I missed my older brother, especially with everything that had been going on—Mom and the tournament.

After he hung up, I crashed on the couch next to Morgan and we watched the remainder of the story about us and our mother. I was glad it didn't make it appear to be a pity party but rather an honor, an opportunity. It didn't hurt we had played so well—by teenage standards, at least—either.

Sleep came easier that night and before I knew it, I was giving my awkward hello to Mr. Mundie and clamoring back into the Escalade. However, the scene that greeted us on the second day was not the same one that greeted us on the first day. The place was crawling with media and fans where we got dropped off, just like the first day.

If I had thought there was a lot of pink and breast cancer support yesterday, I was entirely mistaken. It was all over the place: towels, pink shirts, ribbons, pins, hats. I think I even saw a couple of pairs of pink shoes. As we walked to the putting green, throngs of outstretched arms held items for us to sign. People called us their heroes. Several said they loved us.

"Nothing like a heart throb story, eh boys?" Oberdorf said, grinning back at us but ushering us along all the same. "Try to stay focused."

When Stanley noticed we had arrived at the putting green he jogged over and extended his hand.

"I had no idea," he said. "You dudes are awesome. Sorry I was a grump yesterday. I'm rooting for ya."

We both thanked him and he nodded and went back to where he was stationed.

I guess everybody is rooting for us, I thought.

The putting green was surrounded by an army of pink-clad fans watching us warm up.

"Well I'm about to become the most famous caddy ever, aren't I?" said Tim, as he made his way through the pink sea of fans.

"Not if you're late again, you're not," Oberdorf grumbled.

"You would be the negative, Nancy Obi," Brian said, from his spot a few yards away.

We really shouldn't have been surprised to see the mass that crowded around the first tee when our time was up but we still were. I mean, the most fans I had ever seen prior to yesterday's round was three and they were all family. Nobody had ever watched me play before. Now, thousands were watching.

"Holy shit," Brian said, as he surveyed the scene behind him. "That's a shitload of people."

For some reason, it didn't make me nervous. I felt confident, maybe even cocky. Brian and I had inspired these people. They were here, on this first tee, to see us. They didn't care how well we played; they cared about for what we were playing. They were here for the message and it showed in my game, all day.

I poured in birdies. I pounded drives. I spun wedges and flushed irons. I was an artist and I was creating a damn good piece of art.

"I don't want to touch these clubs right now," Tim said on the 10th tee. "I feel like I'll jinx 'em or taint 'em or something. You grab your own club."

I wasn't about to say no to that. I was on a roll. I shot a 31 on the front nine to get me to 3-under for the tournament. The leader yesterday had finished at 4-under and I couldn't have been far off.

Oberdorf had remained silent for the whole round. He wouldn't dare say anything right now. He was a nervous wreck, biting his nails down to nubs and constantly cracking his knuckles.

"Here comes the collapse," Brian said, as we walked down the 10th fairway. "You know it's happening."

It never did.

I was absolutely on fire. By the 15th hole, I had rolled in two more birdies and I knew I would have no problem making the cut, which was projected to be around 5-over-par. I also began to realize Brian was precariously close to missing it.

He had put together a decent round, better than yesterday at least, but it was still very iffy if he would be playing over the weekend. With four holes to play, he was right on the number. Stanley was already done. He had bogeyed and double-bogeyed, three-putted and hit balls out of bounds. At this point, he was just rooting for us.

"C'mon Bri, you're not gonna let your brother get the best of you, are you," he said, as we walked to the 16th with Brian still on the number.

Brian had begun to realize he was in danger of not making the cut, too. He smiled weakly and tried to say something in return but managed nothing more than some weird stammer a choking sort of noise.

I felt helpless.

The only thing I could do was watch and hope.

I gave my mother, who had been given an "inside the ropes" pass so she could follow us without any trouble, a thumbs up and tried to reassure her but she was a wreck. She buried her head in my dad's chest every time Brian hit a shot, much the same way she watched Colton play football.

Brian bogeyed the 17th to jump to 6-over, one shot back.

I attempted to tell him that 5-over was just a projected cut and it might go up but he just shook his head and let out a string of curses. Not even James could help him out. I couldn't tell who was suffering more from Brian's close call with the cut—my mom, Oberdorf or Brian.

His tee-shot on the 18th hole was pressure-proof and he left himself with about 175 yards from the middle of the fairway. The only problem, though, was the 18th green was tremendously difficult. It was surrounded by water and sloped steeply from front to back. The pin was in the back right corner, tucked behind a deep bunker. It wasn't an inviting placement for an aggressive shot, but Brian had no other option.

If he left it short, he would have an impossible bunker shot. If he went long, he would be wet. Bailing out to the left would leave him with a tough putt but he at least had a chance of making it.

Not trying to throw away the best round of my life, I took the safe road and landed my approach off towards the left about thirty feet from the pin.

Brian was the last player to go.

After a few minutes of intense discussions with James, he pulled out his 7-iron, risking going long in the water rather than leaving it short in the bunker. He stepped back from the ball, ran his hands through his shaggy brown hair and stepped up. From the looks and sounds of things, everybody in the crowd was holding their breath. All you could hear was the breeze whispering through the palms.

I closed my eyes and turned my back.

Then the place exploded. As soon as the ball left Brian's clubs, the crowd erupted.

"Get in the hole."

"It's in."

"Mashed potatoes."

Brian stared it down as it took a line towards the right side of the bunker and began curling back towards the pin. It was right on it. It fell towards the earth and we could tell it was over the bunker but we weren't sure if it went over the green.

I still held my breath.

Then the crowd burst into raucous celebration. Thousands of hands went straight up in the air as if they were signaling a field goal. People were high-fiving and hugging. Brian wasn't satisfied though, not yet. He smiled weakly and waved his hand to the crowd to acknowledge them.

I wanted to say something to him, something to encourage him, lift him, or let him know he was going to make it but sometimes, in golf, the best thing is to say nothing at all. He knew what he had to do. Now it was time to do it.

We couldn't tell how far away his ball was from the pin because the bunker blocked our view. Nevertheless, when we finally arrived, it was clear why the crowd reacted as they did. His ball lay a mere four feet away, just beyond the pin. I could tell from his ball mark at the back edge of the green, he had nearly gone long and spilled into the water but the ball had spun back a good five feet to leave Brian with a tricky slider.

"This is why we did that putting drill every damn day," Oberdorf said, as he passed by me on the green. "That putt right there."

Of course, he was right. Not wanting Brian to have to think about his upcoming putt for too long, I didn't take much time with mine. I rolled it to within a few inches and tapped in for par.

I shot a 65, the best round of my career, a number that might just be the lowest of the whole tournament through two days.

"Excellent round," Oberdorf said, as I walked off.

However, I had never been so unrelieved after playing so well. My heart raced as I watched Brian stalk his four footer. He circled the hole and circled it again, like a vulture preparing to swoop. Finally, he lined up his ball and stepped over it.

The crowd was impossibly quiet, even more stoic than they had been when Brian was hitting his approach shot. Again, I held my breath and turned my back.

I couldn't watch. I didn't have to. The whole place let out one enormous, collective, heart-wrenching "oh…no."

My heart sank. I turned around and first saw Brian, collapsed to his knees on the green, looking painfully at his ball, which had stopped one inch in front of the cup. It may as well have been a mile.

I looked for my mom, who had her hand cupped over her mouth, her eyes wide. My Uncle Tito had turned a beer 90 degrees up. My dad was squatting, hands on his head. Morgan looked at me and put her palms to the sky as if to ask "what happened?" She didn't understand golf and didn't know Brian had likely just missed the cut.

Nevertheless, the crowd erupted louder than it had all day when Brian tapped in for par to finish his first two days at 6-over. Brian then did something I had never seen him do after missing a short putt, especially on the 18th hole—he smiled. He grabbed his ball from the bottom of the cup, examined it for a minute, surveyed the crowd, which was giving him a momentous ovation and flashed a smile, which probably melted thousands of teenage girls' hearts.

He sub-consciously handed his putter to Tim, walked over to where my mother was standing near the front-left side of the green and gave her a long hug.

Cue the crowd.

I saw him mouth the words 'I love you' before he walked past her, signed his scorecard, and began mingling with the crowd.

He signed autographs for hours on that 18th green. He knew the number would never climb to 6-over. He knew his playing days in this tournament were finished but he also knew what his playing meant to our supporters and he wanted to let them know how much he appreciated them.

I signed a few hats and towels and talked for a little while but my mind was busy thinking about the leaderboard. Could I really be close to the top? Could I possibly be vying for a share of the lead at a professional golf tournament?

"It's just you now, Jay," said Oberdorf rather solemnly, as we stared at the towering scoreboard in front of us. "Brian's not getting a miracle. He's done. You're going to have to focus one thousand times more than you have for the first two days. Sure, you have the story and the crowd and all the intangibles on your side. And you're an excellent player but these guys are the best. You can't try to play their game, you need to play yours or you're dead meat."

He was right, of course. I knew that, he knew that, we all knew it. I took a deep breath as the little scorekeeper put a few red numbers next to Nick Eckard's name. He had shot 63 and was 8-under for the tournament.

We would be paired together tomorrow—Nick Eckard and I, the high-schooler and the best player in the world.

CHAPTER 18

It was strange, playing without Brian. I had asked him if he wanted to caddy for me but he declined. He was far more concerned with diving into the lavish amenities available to the players: the free food, the free golf balls and, of course, the high profile image women covet.

"My goal is to get more numbers than what I shot," he said as he popped a chocolate ball into his mouth and turned to make his way over to the fence by the putting green where an attractive blonde was standing and immediately struck up a conversation. That's where he would stay for the remainder of my thirty-minute putting warm-up.

This was without a doubt the most nervous I had ever been for a round of golf. Nothing came even close. The media circus had grown to impossible proportions and the crowd support seemed to triple with every hour. I still couldn't be calmed. I couldn't imagine the train wreck I would've been had Oberdorf not forged my mental game together through his maddening drills.

As on the second day, the amount of people wearing pink grew exponentially. There were breast cancer symbols everywhere. My mother, in fact, was even signing autographs at this point. She tried to shrug them off at first, politely declining and telling the autograph hounds she was here for me but when somebody informed her we were there for her, she gave in.

A representative from Susan G. Komen for the Cure, the giant breast cancer fighting foundation, had asked her to think about becoming a spokesperson and tell her story to a wider audience. Of course, the rep didn't know my mother's days were numbered. Nobody did except for Oberdorf, Morgan and my immediate family. However, she was understanding when my mother declined the offer.

It was certainly nice to have the crowd backing my family and me again but I was playing against the outstanding Nick Eckard. No crowd could soothe these nerves. I had grown up idolizing the guy. He was one of the all-time greats in the sport, yet had an uncanny ability to stay grounded and humble. He played the game with a childlike wonder, not caring if he missed the cut or didn't cash in on a big paycheck. He was just out there having fun. The money came second to him. I admired that.

I had gotten to the first tee a little early and was chatting with a couple men who said they had followed me all thirty-six holes of the tournament and were rooting for me. How could I not talk to them?

But when Eckard walked onto the tee, the place erupted. He was a fan favorite, the media's Golden Boy. They loved him, possibly more than any athlete in any sport. He waved his parade wave and walked his red-carpet walk. He glided over to where I had stationed myself next to the men and held out his hand.

"Love what you've been doing, brother," he said, with a smile. "Love it. Now, I'm not sure if I'd appreciate you kicking my ass or anything but I hope you do well. It's an honor to meet you."

An honor? To meet me? Who was this guy, the golf god, talking about?

"Pleasure's all mine," I said, trying to shake his hand as firmly as I could.

"It's a shame your brother missed the cut. From the looks of things, though, I'd say he's enjoying himself," Eckard laughed, pointing to where Brian was standing amongst a group of attractive blondes in skimpy skirts and low-cut tops.

"He probably missed that putt on purpose," I said, with a chuckle.

Eckard was fun to play with. I had liked Stanley a lot, especially when his mood had improved during the second day but there was just something about Eckard you couldn't help liking. He talked and laughed and made jokes throughout the whole round. He chatted with a few fans on every tee box and waved to the crowd every time he finished out a hole.

"If you continue your golf career, that's your guy to model it after," said Oberdorf, as we made the turn and Eckard was walking and signing autographs the whole way to the 10th tee. "He's a guy every father wants his daughter to date."

I had never been one to show much emotion, especially not on the golf course. However, as I watched my thirty-foot putt for birdie on No. 10 disappear into the cup, I lost control. I leaned my head back and let out a roar silenced by the deafening explosion of the crowd. I flipped my putter over to Tim and unleashed a series of violent fist pumps as I swaggered around the green. I waved my hands into the air for the crowd to grow even louder. They did. I didn't stop screaming and fist pumping and pointing at random people in the gallery until Oberdorf motioned for me to calm down.

I had never felt something like this before. The electricity. The rush. The grandeur of the moment.

It was incredible.

I took in huge breaths of air to slow my heart but the adrenaline coursing through my veins wouldn't allow it. I don't know what it was about that putt but it set off a time bomb that had been sitting in my stomach since the day my mother told me about her cancer. It had fed off all of my pent up emotions and the birdie putt had finally ignited a fire in me.

For the rest of that round, I was a crazed man. Eckard just went about his business as usual and the fans were polite to him. It was nothing like the support they were showing for me, though. People reached over the ropes to clap me on the back between every hole. Applause greeted me on every tee box, standing ovations on every green. No matter the size of the putt or the length of the drive, they reacted like I had just won the Masters. They cheered and laughed and boomed with applause.

I played to it. I screamed and yelled and hollered and fist pumped. I shook my hands in the air with every birdie dropped and par saved. I was on some kind of high. I didn't want to come down.

"You're a crazy mother," Eckard laughed as we shook hands on the 18th green. "In all my years, I've never seen anything like this. You deserve it, you're whole family. I'll be seeing you tomorrow."

He gave me an encouraging pat on the chest, walked off the green and disappeared into the masses. I looked around at the scene in front of me.

I saw the grandstands behind the green, filled with beaming faces of people I didn't know. I saw the people behind the ropes on either side of the green, clapping emphatically and chanting my name. Then I saw the one face that really mattered—my mother's. It brought it all back to reality.

I called her over to the center of the green. She looked confused. "Me?" she mouthed, looking around and pointing at Brian and Morgan and my dad and Uncle Tito and Oberdorf.

"Me?" she asked again.

I nodded and waved her forward. As she stepped onto the green and made her way over, I heard, still to this day, the most deafening sound I have ever heard in my entire life. It was as if somebody had actually placed a block of C4 and detonated it right on the spot.

When my mother reached me in the center of the green, I wrapped her up in the tightest hug I'd ever given anybody.

Another explosion.

"I love you, Ma," I screamed into her ear. She was shaking, although I wasn't sure if she was crying or if it was the vibrations from the crowd's earsplitting response. She just hugged me tight. I handed her the ball I had played with the whole round and motioned for her to throw it into the crowd. She half-laughed, half-cried and wound up her right arm and tossed it into the screaming mass. They scrambled for the ball. We walked off the green. I wouldn't come down from that moment until hours after. Morgan and I held hands as we walked on the beach near the ocean so the water would lap at our feet every now and then. It was just us and a few unknowing passersby. We didn't really say a word to each other. We just walked, hand-in-hand, in silence. At that particular moment, I wouldn't have wanted anything else. She leaned her head on my shoulder as we made our way down the cool beach. The sun was setting on another beautiful, perfect, California day.

I stopped and plopped down, not minding getting my shorts soaked in the freezing ocean. For about an hour, Morgan and I just watched in silence as the sun slowly disappeared below the horizon in a portrait of magnificent reds and yellows and oranges.

"You know," I finally said, taking Morgan's hand and examining it. "Tomorrow isn't going to be like today. Everything is going to change tomorrow. Everything will change for the rest of my life."

She nodded and replaced her head back on my shoulder.

"I know."

"Tomorrow," I said, kissing her hand. "Is going to be the last 18 holes of golf my mother will ever see. Tomorrow is it."

Morgan lifted her head off my shoulder and stood, helping me up in the process. She hugged me tight and kissed me on the cheek.

"Then you should get some rest," she said. "You're going to want to give her a good story to take to Heaven with her."

CHAPTER 19

I had known for a long time the day would come when my mother's struggle would end. I just didn't know when. But there was something different about that Sunday, the final day of the tournament. I felt it when I woke up. I felt it in my bones, my nerves, in the very air I breathed and the food I ate. Nobody spoke in the morning. We ate breakfast in silence. Even my Uncle Tito didn't say a word.

He didn't even crack a beer.

Oberdorf wanted me to get to the course extra early but I waved him off. For some reason I didn't care much for the tournament right now. I was just two shots back from Eckard and had earned a spot in the final pairing with him again but it seemed so insignificant, so small.

Instead, I went back down to the beach, the one place where I could get some peace, clear my mind. That place used to be the golf course. My world had flipped itself inside out these past couple weeks and that was something with which I knew I would have to deal. I just stared into the ocean and watched as the surf inhaled and exhaled onto the sand. The sound of the waves crashing was calming to me. I no longer felt the nerves of playing in front of the gallery, but there was still a restlessness in my insides, which I couldn't calm.

Brian felt it, too.

I don't know how long he had been standing next to me but I nearly jumped out of my drawers when he spoke.

"It's weird, today," he said. "Something's...different. I don't know how to explain it."

"I know," I said. "I feel it too."

We stood there for a while, each of us getting lost in our thoughts before he said I only had an hour before my tee time.

"I guess this is it then," I breathed.

He nodded. We walked back to the hotel.

Oberdorf was fuming but even he could tell something was off with me.

"You Boys," he had begun, before catching the sight of our faces. "Alright then, let's go at your pace. Tell me when you want to go."

I loved Oberdorf for that. He was as tough as any military man but he was also one of the more understanding men I'd ever meet. Oberdorf had laid out a blue polo for me to wear, which the tournament sponsors had chosen for me.

I had other plans. I reached into my bag and pulled out a light pink shirt. The right sleeve had my mother's initials emblazoned on either side of a white breast cancer ribbon and there was another breast cancer logo above my heart. Morgan had made it specifically for the tournament.

"I'll pay whatever the fine is," I said, when Oberdorf began to interject.

"Pink looks better on you, anyway," he said. "Don't worry about the sponsors, they'll love it."

Even Mr. Mundie seemed to realize I was in no mood for chiding today. The hulking, tattooed man even wished me luck—and not just to break 100—as I stepped out of the Escalade.

I'm not sure if the fans expected me to put on the circus act I had yesterday but, if they did, they didn't really show it. As always, they cheered loudly and took every opportunity to clap me on the back or shake my hand. This time, however, I just nodded politely, put my head down, and made my way to wherever it was I was going.

My swing felt as smooth as ever on the driving range and my putting was still infallible on the practice green, but when your heart and mind are just not into a round, they just aren't into it. You lose focus, you make tiny mistakes you normally wouldn't make.

"Talk to me," said Oberdorf, as he pulled me off the first tee before the round was to begin. "What's going on with you? I know something's not quite right so don't bullshit me."

I thought for a minute, kicking the perfectly manicured grass below me.

"This is it, Obi," I finally said. "This is it. The last round. This is the last round she'll ever see."

Oberdorf sighed.

"Look, I wish I knew how you feel but I don't and I'm no good at these speeches," he said, "But I'll tell you what I do know. I know there's no other way your mother would rather spend her last hours on this wonderful earth than to watch you or Brian play golf. She's with family, friends, people who love her. She's doing what she has wanted to do since you first picked up a club and that's see you out here. Have you ever seen her as happy as she has been these past couple days? She's the happiest damn woman on the planet. What you need to do, right now, for the next four hours, is honor her. Play in her memory. Don't feel sorry for yourself or for her. Worse things happen every day. Consider yourself lucky that you have this God-given talent you can use to make her last days the happiest of her entire life."

He was right.

I nodded, lips pursed, confidence back. That icy pit in my stomach had been filled with warmth. The fog that had plagued my mind was lifted. Everything was clear again.

"You OK, buddy?" Eckard asked, as I reemerged onto the tee.

"Yeah, just needed a minute," I said. "This is a little different than a high school tournament, you know."

He laughed and clapped me on the back.

"Go get 'em."

I was a machine all day—methodical, practiced and unwavering. I wasn't the hair-raising phenomena I was yesterday. I didn't let emotions overwhelm me or the adrenaline consume me. I simply went about my business.

I birdied three holes on the front nine while bogeying none. At the turn, I was tied with Eckard for the lead.

"Dude," said Tim, as he handed me my driver on the 10th hole. "You can actually do this."

"I know."

Age be damned, this was something I could do. It was something I had to do.

However, Eckard was a damn good golfer and he wasn't about to let some kid—no matter how inspirational and heart-warming the story—take him down. He rooted for me to do well and I truly think he meant it, because he would rather win a tournament than have somebody else lose one.

I was forcing him to do that.

He birdied the 11th and I countered with one of my own on the 12th. We each made pars on the next two holes and then he drained a dagger of a putt on the 15th. What I thought was an impossible putt, he apparently saw as a good birdie opportunity. He was staring at a 60-foot downhill slider with at least 10 feet of break and, I have to hand it to the guy, he played it perfectly. It dropped into the cup with a little 'dink' just to confirm it really had gone in and the crowd let out a roar.

I just smiled ,clapped and cheered with them.

"That's why you're the best, Nick," I said.

My 15-footer missed. The crowd gasped.

I tapped in for a par with no shame whatsoever. Two more pars on the 16th and 17th left me one back with one hole to go.

I know I've described it before but the 18th hole at Olympiad Golf Club is a monster at its most modest description. A 525-yard par-4 that dives left and then back to the right. The fairways are guarded by towering palm trees and water forms a crescent around either side of the green. Then, when you've finally made it to the green, that's just as precarious as the journey to it.

It has a steep slope on the right side, feeding into the back of the green, which conveniently encourages balls to run off the end and sink into the water. The left side is less worrisome but, then again, miss a hair on the near side and the ball is in for another watery landing.

Just twenty birdies had been made on the hole in all four days, up to this point. That's 320 attempts without a birdie on the hole this week. I had never tried for one. It was foolish and stupid.

The 18th was not a hole at which to make up strokes. It was a hole to survive. Now I had to win it. I had to make a birdie.

Eckard was too good and too smart to play aggressively here. He wouldn't risk making bogey or worse. When he pulled out his 3-wood on the tee I knew I had predicted accurately. He took his pendulum-smooth swing and pounded one down the middle of the fairway.

He still had a long way into the green but he would likely hit it short and give himself a pretty easy up-and-down to make. Worst comes to worst, I make par and he makes bogey and we go to extra holes. I didn't like my chances there.

I motioned for Tim to pull out my driver and, unlike the first day in which he protested to no end until I gave in and decided on 3-wood, he silently handed it to me.

The crowd was dead silent.

I closed my eyes and tried to imagine the sounds of the crashing waves on the shore and the smell of the salty sea. I smiled to myself as I remembered the serenity of this morning. My heartbeat slowed back to normal. My hands stopped shaking. I reopened my eyes, took the club back and ripped it through. I didn't even watch the ball for a second. I knew I wouldn't have to. From what Tim told me, it had begun on a line down the left side, just over the trees, and drew ever so slightly back in, cutting the corner perfectly and leaving me with as short a shot in as I could possibly get. God, I loved that ball flight.

If it were yesterday, I would have embellished the shot. I would have run around, high-fiving the fans and waving for them to grow louder. I would have screamed and fist-pumped, used the shot to grab the momentum but this wasn't yesterday. I was playing for something much more today.

Eckard got to his ball and did exactly what I had thought he would do. His iron trickled down just short of the green and he would have a pretty easy pitch to where the pin was positioned in the back left corner.

My mind went back to the beach. I could hear the wind whispering through the palms and the occasional murmur of someone in the crowd but my mind was far from the golf course.

I stepped back from the ball and looked for my family. There they stood, all linking arms for good luck, smiling tensely. I grinned and nodded and approached the ball again. I had just an 8-iron into the green, an easy shot.

The club ripped through the grass so easily I hardly felt it hit the ball. There was nothing but silence as it floated toward the left edge of the green, hovering ever so slightly over the water before beginning its slight curve back and diving two feet next to the pin before sucking back about six feet in front of it.

The crowd went absolutely insane, nuts, bananas. I turned and handed my club to Tim and he began to walk toward the green but I put my hand on his shoulder to stop him.

"Tim, I love you buddy, but let me take them just this once," I said.

He looked confused but handed my clubs over, nonetheless.

"Go get my family and bring 'em out here."

A look of understanding crossed his face.

"You're an inspiration, you know that?" he shouted over the crowd's incessant applause. "You've changed a lot of lives this week."

"You helped me the whole way," I shouted.

Tears were beginning to well in my eyes. He smiled, squeezed my shoulder and jogged over to where my family was standing. He whispered in Brian's ear and my brother grinned and out they came—Uncle Tito, Brian, Morgan, my father. My mother.

"Let me take these for you, big fella," said Uncle Tito, slinging my bag onto his thick shoulder.

My mother didn't say anything. She just hugged me tight. The crowd whistled, clapped, cheered and cried.

So, we walked—my family and I—down the 18th fairway. A six-foot putt for a 17-year-old kid to either win or send a tournament to extra holes hung in the balance. I couldn't have cared less.

I slung a lanky arm around my mother. And, for one last time, to the roars and cheers of the crowd, we walked down the fairway together.

Four days after the tournament ended, my mother passed away.

EPILOGUE

After it was all said and done, after the media vans packed and left, after the grandstands were taken down and the course returned to normal, after Oberdorf had taken his flight home, Brian and I stood on the 18th green.

We looked at the water and said no words, because what words could ever describe what we had just accomplished?

We had taken the golfing world by storm. We had captured the heart of a nation, inspired thousands, maybe millions.

He didn't say anything when he walked off the green. He just hugged me, patted me on the back and disappeared into the night.

But I couldn't leave the place that changed my life forever. I didn't pick up a golf club a single time for the rest of my life. Brian tried to convince me it would be in Mom's honor to play but I couldn't do it. There was just something about the game that kept me from picking it back up. Maybe someday I'll play again, I doubt it.

Brian, meanwhile, had gone on to play for Alcorn and still plays professionally, today. He has won his fair share of tournaments, started a family of his own and tells our story to his own kids from time to time.

I married Morgan when I was still in college. I did go to Alcorn, just not to play golf. We now have two kids of our own, Jocelyn and Matthew. They have found a knack for the game I once loved. I never thought I'd understand the joy my mother got when she watched us play, but now I know. There was nothing more I ever wanted to do other than watch my kids play.

But now, as I walk through Olympiad as I do on every anniversary of that Sunday, so many years ago, my heart warms as it always does. I brush my hands on the palm trees I once hated. I sit in the bunkers I once loathed. I study the greens that gave me so much angst.

It all brings it back. I open my arms to the sky and look up, because I know she is watching and thinking about that day, that day when she watched her boy play the last 18 holes of golf he would ever play.

I smile to myself, shake my head, blow a kiss to the heavens and walk off the green.

What a story this is to tell.

ABOUT THE AUTHOR

Travis Mewhirter is a 24-year-old sportswriter currently living in Navarre, Fla. with his wolfdog, Sam, writing prep and college sports for the Northwest Florida Daily News. A 2012 graduate of the University of Maryland's Philip Merrill College of Journalism, he has previously been a PGA Tour columnist for Yahoo! Sports and a sportswriter for The Washington Post. You can contact him through email at tmewhirter@nwfdailynews.com or twitter @TravisMWnwfdn

Made in the USA
San Bernardino, CA
01 October 2018